FIGHTING HEALTH INSURANCE DENIALS

A Primer for Lawyers

SCOTT GLOVSKY, ESQ.

ISBN: 0692568824
ISBN-13: 978-0692568828

DEDICATION

To Mariana, Xabi and Matthew. Thank you for your love. If you believe in yourself and try your best, you can accomplish anything.

To my colleagues Ari Dybnis, Roberta Liao and Al Heath. This book would not exist without your hard work. Thank you for helping our clients get justice every day.

DISCLAIMER

This book is intended as an educational source for practicing lawyers. This book does not offer any legal advice and does not replace a consultation with a lawyer. Attorneys are strongly advised to evaluate the information, ideas, analysis, and opinions set forth in this book, but to also conduct their own research into applicable statutes, regulations, case law and rules. Attorneys are also strongly advised to reach their own conclusions and to make independent decisions based on their own experience and research, whether it is consistent or not with the information presented in this book.

Quotations from and citations to cases may not be suitable for use in litigation in any particular case. The law set forth in this book may not reflect the current state of the law as the law is constantly changing. For this reason, attorneys should always conduct their own research and rely upon that before relying upon the information in this book.

All references to trademarks of third parties are strictly informational and for the purposes of commentary only. No sponsorship or endorsement by, or affiliation with, the trademark owners is claimed or implied by the author or publisher of this book. The author and publisher disclaim any liability or responsibility for loss or damage resulting from the use of this book or the information, ideas and opinions contained in this book.

CONTENTS

CONTENTS (Cont'd)

CONTENTS (Cont'd)

CONTENTS (Cont'd)

INTRODUCTION

I have had the privilege of spending most of my career representing people in lawsuits against health insurance companies that deny them medical care. My clients are everyday people who have paid their hard-earned money to insurance companies to protect them in the unfortunate event that they become ill. They trusted their insurers and believed their marketing promises touting quality health care. But time and time again, I have seen billion-dollar insurance companies wrongly deny medical treatment to good people who are fighting serious illnesses. The insurers pay ivory tower law firms millions of dollars to defend their improper denials.

The fights against health insurers are not easy, and the obstacles are numerous. For example, most people have virtually no rights to sue their health insurers for denying medical care due to the limits of the Employee Retirement Income Security Act of 1974 ("ERISA"). For people who are not limited by ERISA, primarily those who purchase their insurance directly from health insurers, government employees, Obamacare recipients, or Medicare recipients, they almost certainly have unknowingly signed arbitration agreements through which they ostensibly have waived their right to sue their insurer in court. Instead, they are required to pursue their claims in arbitration – which is costly, secretive and often unfair.

But these are worthy fights. We need to wage these battles to protect our clients and the people in our communities. Health insurers are in business to make money, and they make more money when they deny care to their members.

I acknowledge at the outset that I am biased. I have seen too many people betrayed by their insurance companies. In these pages I seek to arm my colleagues with strategies to win these cases.

As a trial lawyer, I am a storyteller. So in addition to exploring litigation strategy, in these pages I explore how to develop and tell powerful stories. I am particularly grateful to Gerry Spence and his Trial Lawyers College for teaching me most of what I know about storytelling.

I am very proud that some of my cases have led insurance companies to change their practices and stop systemically denying certain medical treatments. I am hopeful that my experiences will help you fight for your clients to receive the medical care that they need and that together we can limit the health insurers' practice of putting profits over people's lives.

Good luck.

SECTION I: INSURANCE BASICS

Chapter 1: Different Types of Health Insurance

If your client has health insurance, he or she almost certainly receives coverage through a health insurer, a managed health care plan, a self-insured plan, or a government program. Health insurers often provide both health insurance plans and managed care plans through different subsidiaries. For example, Anthem Blue Cross of California sells both health insurance and managed care plans.

Managed Care Plans

There are substantial differences between health insurance plans and managed care plans. Managed care plans often take the form of health maintenance organizations (commonly referred to as an "HMO"). Under an HMO, a subscriber agrees to pay a monthly premium to the managed care plan in exchange for a network of health care providers who can provide care at no additional cost or at a reduced cost.[1] Under an HMO, the member is generally limited to the providers in the network. Because of this limit, a subscriber must reside in a geographic area that the plan services. Members are generally required to get a referral from their general practitioner to access specialists. These plans take out a lot of the hassle of finding doctors, but members of these plans have little flexibility to choose doctors. These plans generally employ a bureaucratic network through which a subscriber must navigate to get referrals for specialists. Kaiser plans are examples of HMO plans.

Other managed care plans include Preferred Provider Organization ("PPO") and Exclusive Provider Organization ("EPO") plans. In PPO plans, members can access a network of contracted providers on a low or no cost basis. However, these members often have the ability to obtain partially covered treatment from out-of-network providers. Members can generally see any doctor and still receive some minimal coverage for the treatment.

EPO plans function like HMO plans. EPO plan members are restricted to doctors within their EPO network and generally receive no coverage for out-of-network care. However, in contrast to HMOs, EPOs allow members to seek services from specialists within their network without the need for a referral from their general practitioner.

The simplest way to determine what type of policy or plan your client has is to check their enrollment form or their insurance contract. An enrollment form is a document that one signs to enroll in a plan. The form should clearly state the name and type of plan.

Traditional Health Insurance

Health insurance companies traditionally offer policies where consumers pay a monthly premium in exchange for health care coverage. Historically, when an insured needed medical care, they were able to choose their own provider and were not limited by a specific network. Since health insurance provided coverage through any provider, the insureds were not limited by geographic coverage areas as they were with managed care plans.

Self-Insured Plans

A self-insured group health plan is one in which an employer assumes an obligation to provide coverage for the health care needs of its employees. This means that self-insured employers agree to pay for each out-of-pocket employee claim for health care coverage as the claims arise. Self-insured employers will either manage such claims themselves, or subcontract this service to a third party administrator. Third party administrators can be health plans. This can cause confusion by employees as to whether they have a self-insured plan or a managed care plan. A way to easily resolve this confusion, as explained above, is for the employee to check their enrollment form or insurance contract.

A self-insured health plan can follow the structure of either a traditional insurance plan or a managed care plan. The choice of how the plan operates is left to each particular employer.

Government Plans

There are three basic types of government health care plans: Medicare, Medicaid, and Veterans Affairs' plans. Medicare is the federal health insurance program for people 65 or older, certain younger people with disabilities, and people with End-Stage Renal Disease (permanent kidney failure requiring dialysis or a transplant, sometimes called ESRD).

Medicaid is a health care program for individuals and families with low incomes and few resources. The program is federally funded but each state is left to establish its own eligibility standards, determine the type and scope of services covered, set rates of payment for the services, and administer the program. In California, the Medicaid program is called Medi-Cal.

The United States Department of Veterans Affairs provides patient care and federal benefits to veterans and their dependents.

Since government programs are mostly governed by regulation and statute, eligibility requirements and plan benefits are often clearly delineated by the government. Further, the health care coverage is almost always restricted to health care practitioners with whom the government contracts to provide services to plan members. So for example, a Medicare recipient can only receive covered care from a doctor who has contracted with the government to provide care to Medicare recipients at specific rates.

Medicare has a variety of plans, including plans that it offers through private insurers it contracts with to provide benefits to members. These plans are known as Medicare Advantage Plans. Such plans are very similar to private healthcare plans as they can be HMOs and PPOs. Additionally, they can take the form of Private Fee for Service ("PFFS") plans, Special Needs Plans ("SNP"), HMO Point of Service ("HMOPOS") plans, and Medical Savings Account ("MSA") plans.

A PFFS is a plan which gives beneficiaries the right to go to any contracted provider or institution for treatment. In a PFFS plan, Medicare pays a set amount each month per member to a private insurance company and the insurance company pays on a fee-for-service basis for all medical services that the insured needs. An SNP is a plan for people with certain diseases or conditions. The plan provides coverage for hospital stays, office visits, prescription drugs, and all other Medicare-covered services. An SNP tailors benefits, doctors, and drug coverage to meet the specific needs of the member. An HMOPOS is an HMO plan which allows members to get some services out of network at a higher out-of-pocket cost to the insured. Finally, an MSA plan is one that acts as a bank account into which Medicare deposits money for medical services. The insured can use this money during the year to pay for all necessary medical services. The downside of MSA plans is that they typically bear a very high deductible.

Chapter 2: Understanding Consumer Rights to Identify Violations

An insured's rights are dictated by a combination of the law and the terms of their policy. Federal and state laws require health insurers to provide minimum policy benefits. Under the Patient Protection and Affordable Care Act (commonly referred to as "Obamacare"), these basic minimum benefits are referred to as "essential health benefits." These benefits are as follows: ambulatory patient services; emergency services; hospitalization; maternity and newborn care; mental health and substance use disorder services, including behavioral health treatment; prescription drugs; rehabilitative and habilitative services and devices; laboratory services; preventive and wellness services and chronic disease management; and pediatric services, including oral and vision care.

The best place to look for the specific benefits to which your client is entitled is in their Evidence of Coverage. This document contains the terms of the contract that your client entered into with the insurer.

Aside from the explicit terms in the Evidence of

Coverage, there are many benefits to which a member may be entitled under California law. Health plans will often deny coverage for such benefits despite the fact that they are required to cover them. For example, this commonly happens when a consumer seeks mental health treatment.

In 1999, the California legislature passed a law most commonly referred to as the Mental Health Parity Act. The act requires health plans and health insurance companies to provide coverage for the diagnosis and treatment of people with severe mental illness under the same terms that they apply to other medical conditions. Such severe mental illnesses include: schizophrenia; schizoaffective disorder; bipolar disorder (manic-depressive illness); major depressive disorders; panic disorder; obsessive-compulsive disorder; pervasive developmental disorder or autism; anorexia nervosa; and bulimia nervosa.

This law requires health insurance companies to provide treatment for persons with severe mental illness, regardless of whether or not that person's policy explicitly states that the policy provides such coverage. Despite this law, many health insurers systemically and wrongfully told insureds that certain mental health treatments are not covered.

For example, I have represented parents of children with Autism Spectrum Disorders seeking medically necessary behavioral therapy from large health plans. During the course of these lawsuits, I learned that certain health plans systemically claimed that behavioral therapy was not covered. However, under the Mental Health Parity Act, coverage was required. For this reason, it is important to know your clients' rights and to not accept on its face any denials of coverage.

If your client has a government-run health insurance plan, then there are resources to review for their benefits in addition to state and federal law and the Evidence of

Coverage. Specifically, review the website for the government agency administering your client's plan. For example, to understand your client's Medicare benefits, the best resource is Medicare.gov; to understand your client's Veterans Affairs benefits, the best place to look is VA.gov; and to understand your client's Medi-Cal benefits, the best place to look is http://www.dhcs.ca.gov/services/medi-cal/Pages/MediBen_Svcs.aspx.

Chapter 3: Medical Necessity

Whether your client has a health insurance policy or is a member of a health plan, medical necessity is a prerequisite for coverage for all treatment. This is true regardless of whether they are in a PPO, EPO or HMO. If an insured seeks coverage for a service that the insurer does not consider medically necessary, then the insurer will deny coverage. This applies whether an insured seeks coverage before or after a medical service is performed. This is why it is important to understand what medical necessity means.

"Medical Necessity" includes health care services or supplies that a healthcare worker provides for the purpose of evaluating, diagnosing or treating an illness, injury, disease or its symptoms, in accordance with the generally accepted standards of medical practice. Such services or supplies must be clinically appropriate in terms of type, frequency, extent, site and duration, and not merely cosmetic or convenient for the patient or healthcare provider. "Generally accepted standards of medical practice" are standards based on credible scientific evidence published in peer-reviewed medical literature generally recognized by the relevant medical community and are accepted by other healthcare workers in the community.

Insurance companies have different definitions of medical necessity. For this reason, it is always important to check a plan or policy for the relevant definition. Insurance companies and their medical directors determine whether a service or supply is medically necessary, even if their determination is contrary to the determination of a patient's doctor.

It is also important to note that medically beneficial is not synonymous with medically necessary. In other words, just because a procedure might treat a condition that a person has, it does not mean that the procedure is "medically necessary" under the contract. For example, if a less invasive and less expensive procedure which can treat a symptom is available, then a more costly and advanced procedure for treatment of that same symptom may not be medically necessary.

Similarly, an inpatient hospitalization for treatment will not be medically necessary if the treatment can be provided adequately in an outpatient setting. The most common types of medical procedures that insurers deny as not medically necessary include cosmetic and purely elective surgeries. These include procedures such as Botox injections, hair transplants, and plastic surgery. This being said, there are certain cosmetic procedures that are medically necessary such as reconstructive surgery to restore appearance after a medical illness (i.e. breast reconstruction surgery after breast cancer).

Understanding "medical necessity" is crucial to knowing which procedures or supplies an insurer might cover or pre-authorize. Without an understanding of "medical necessity," consumers risk seeking expensive treatments which they will ultimately have to pay for despite the fact that they have an insurance policy. Regardless, insurers frequently wrongfully deny treatment as not medically necessary.

Chapter 4: What to Do After a Denial

The first step is to gather all information and documents about the claim or treatment denial. Have your client document all communications that he or she has had with the insurer. Collect copies of all letters that the insurer sent and all letters that your client sent to the insurer. If your client had any phone conversations with the insurer, be sure to keep a log of the time and date of the conversation, the name, title, and/or employee identification number of the person your client spoke with, and a description of everything that was said during the conversation. If the client is having trouble remembering such specific information, then they can use their phone bill as a reminder of the time, date, and duration of such phone calls. In the best case scenario, they should record such phone calls, but this usually is not feasible for the average person. It is also necessary for the client to collect as much medical evidence concerning the need for the treatment at issue as possible. This means gathering copies of their medical records and all referrals from health care professionals.

If there is no written denial letter explaining the basis for the denial, then your client must request one. They must be persistent and hold their ground when dealing with the insurer's representatives. It is important that they learn the complete basis for the denial and have the insurer issue a written denial letter.

In some cases, the insurer will take the insidious approach of denying coverage by simply stalling, cancelling all scheduled appointments for treatment, or refusing to schedule appointments for the treatment in the first place. In such situations, the insurer will not admit that they are denying treatment, so they will not provide a written denial. The best approach in such situations is to ask your client create a log noting each time they asked for an appointment, to whom they made the request, the response, the nature of the requested appointment, and each time the insurer cancelled an appointment for treatment. Once you have all of the information surrounding the policy and the denial, you are ready to begin fighting the denial.

Chapter 5: Internal Appeals Process is Available but Generally Not Necessary

The law requires that insurance companies have internal appeal processes. But before you appeal, learn about the appeal process of your specific insurance company. With the exception of ERISA-governed policies, which will be discussed in proceeding chapters, an internal appeal is not necessary to seek relief in court. In many cases it will be futile and an unnecessary delay to file an internal appeal if an insurer has already made their position regarding a denial clear. Further, it is also an option in certain exigent circumstances to skip an internal appeal and seek an independent medical review, though such a step can have its own potentially negative consequences, as explained in the next chapter.

If it is constructive to seek an internal appeal, then it is important to know that each insurance company has a different internal appeal procedure. If your client chooses to appeal, you need to determine the appeals process and have your client follow it. If you write an appeal letter, include your client's name, contact information such as their address and phone number, and information about their policy including the policy number, the group number, and the claim number. You should also include as much written evidence as you have like doctors letters and medical records.

It is crucial to submit as much evidence as possible from physicians and other health care providers specifying why the treatment is medically necessary and why the denial is improper. It is important to keep in mind that many companies have time limits for their internal appeal process. When your client receives a denial, they should immediately look into the time requirements for the internal appeal process so that they can determine when they have to file an appeal, should they choose to do so.

In California, an insured must file such an appeal within 180 days of receiving a denial. Normally, the insurers will determine the merits of an appeal of a pre-authorization denial within thirty days. In urgent situations, an insured can seek an expedited appeal. Expedited appeals are necessary where the insured will suffer harm if the treatment sought is not provided immediately. When an insured files an expedited appeal, the insurer generally has 3 business days to provide a decision on the appeal. Such a decision can be given orally to the insured, but the insurer must then send a written notice of the decision within 48 hours.

Chapter 6: Should You Get an Independent Medical Review?

It is possible that after the internal appeal process, the health plan might reverse their earlier denial. However, if it does not, then in California insureds have a right to have their claim reviewed by an independent body under certain circumstances. An independent review can be incredibly helpful in getting the coverage denial changed, but it is not something that your client should automatically consider since it is generally not a prerequisite for seeking court intervention because of the bad faith denial. In some circumstances, it can be more efficient and beneficial to skip the independent review and simply file a lawsuit.

If you decide that the best move is to seek an external review, determine the proper entity from which you should seek the review. In California, the proper entity is determined by the type of coverage that your client has. If the client has a managed health care plan, you can seek a review from the Department of Managed Health Care ("DMHC"). If your client is covered by a health insurer, you can seek a review from the California Department of Insurance ("CDI"). Both the DOI and the DMHC have similar appeal procedures.

After determining whether the claim is regulated by the DMHC or the CDI, you should visit the website for the particular agency that governs the claims' external appeal. The DMHC website can be found at: http://www.dmhc.ca.gov/dmhc_consumer/pc/pc_forms.aspx. You can also call the DMHC at 1-888-466-2219. The website for the CDI is http://www.insurance.ca.gov/0100-consumers/0020-health-related/0010-consumer-provider-complaints/. You can also reach the CDI by calling them at 800-927-HELP (4357). Both the DMHC and CDI have detailed information on filing a complaint for an external appeal, but in general, the information your client provides them will mirror the information and documents you provide the insurance company or health plan when seeking an internal appeal.

Depending on the reason for the claim denial, you can either file a complaint with the CDI or DMHC or request an independent medical review ("IMR"). An IMR is a free review of an insured by an independent medical professional to determine if a medical decision made by an insurance company was justified and reasonable. An insured can seek an IMR only if their insurance company denied, changed, or delayed a service or treatment because of a finding by the insurance company that the treatment or service was not "medically necessary," their insurance company will not pay for an experimental or investigational treatment for a serious medical condition, or their insurance company refuses to pay for emergency or urgent medical services that the insured has already received.

In conducting an IMR, the independent medical professionals rely upon a variety of sources to craft an opinion on each particular case. Specifically, the professionals rely upon peer-reviewed scientific and medical evidence concerning the disputed health care service, upon the standards for medical professionals that the national community of medical professionals recognize, and upon their own and others' expert opinions. By looking to these sources of information, the independent medical professionals attempt to discern which treatments are likely to be effective and which treatments are not.

Once an insured has completed an IMR application, they must give written consent to allow IMR medical professionals to obtain all necessary medical records. If the IMR application qualifies for an IMR review, then the CDI sends the case to an IMR organization and requests all necessary information from the insurance company at issue. At this point, the IMR organization must complete its review within 30 days. The IMR organization will issue its determination in writing to the insured, the insurance company and to the insurance commissioner. The written determinations will include in-depth findings and descriptions of the insured's medical condition and the important documents the IMR professional used to reach the decision.

In special circumstances, an insured can even completely skip their insurance company's internal grievance process and directly apply to the CDI or DMHC for an IMR. The CDI and DMHC will waive such a requirement when an "extraordinary or compelling" circumstance exists. Such circumstances include, but are not limited to, instances when an insured is in serious pain, has a risk of loss of life, limb, or major bodily function, or has a risk of immediate and serious deterioration of health. If such a circumstance exists, then the CDI must complete the IMR determination within 3 days of receiving the insured's case information. California law also requires that the insured's insurance company deliver all necessary information and documents to the CDI within 24 hours of the expedited IMR request.

If the IMR determines that the insurance company acted improperly, then the CDI or DMHC will issue a written decision compelling the insurance company to change its conduct. This being said, if the IMR determination is adverse to the insured, then it would not preclude the insured from seeking relief for treatment which can still be "medically necessary"--even if the IMR professional came to a contrary determination.

Chapter 7: Medicare Appeals Process

Medicare plans are not only unique in their structure, as described earlier, but also require unique actions when a member experiences a denial. There is a five-step process for appealing a Medicare denial. The majority of these steps are governed by 20 CFR § 422.10, 42 CFR § 405.72 et seq. and § 417.600 et seq. which require that Medicare enrollees who wish to challenge a denial of benefits must exhaust all administrative processes provided by the Centers for Medicare and Medicaid ("CMS", formerly the Health Care Financing Administration ["HCFA"]).

The first step is for a Medicare beneficiary to seek redetermination by the Medicare contractors. In a redetermination, the contractor charged by Medicare for handling the claims for its plan runs through the same process that it implemented to determine the denial, but the process is run by different personnel. Any individual who seeks redetermination has 120 days from the day that they receive the initial denial. Generally, the contractors will then send the member a Medicare Redetermination notice within 60 days after it receives the request for a redetermination.

Should the redetermination result in upholding the denial,

a member next has the right to seek a reconsideration within 180 days of the redetermination. A reconsideration is a process conducted by a Qualified Independent Contractor ("QIC"). These reviews are similar to an IMR as they allow for an independent medical necessity review by doctors who are not associated with the contractor who initially issued the denial. QICs will send decisions to the member who sought reconsideration generally within 60 days of receipt of the request for reconsideration.

The next level of review is available only to those who meet a certain threshold amount of disputed coverage. This amount in controversy changes each year as the medical care component of the consumer price index ("CPI") rises. If the amount in controversy requirement is satisfied, then a Medicare beneficiary can request a review by an Administrative Law Judge ("ALJ"). The ALJ will then hold a live hearing, either by phone or video-teleconference, within 60 days from the date that the ALJ receives the request. If a beneficiary has good cause, they can also request an in-person hearing, though it is up to the ALJ's discretion whether to hold an in-person hearing. ALJs will generally send a decision within 90 days of the date that the beneficiary requests a hearing.

If an ALJ does not overturn the denial, then the Medicare beneficiary can move to the fourth level of review which is to request a review by the Medicare Appeals Council. Such a request must be made in writing within 60 days after the beneficiary receives the ALJ's decision. The Medicare Appeals Council will then review all of the facts of the dispute independent of the previous rulings and will generally issue a decision within 90 days.

It is only after review by the Medicare Appeals Council and only in cases in which a specific amount in controversy is met that a Medicare beneficiary can seek relief from a claim denial by a judge in a United States District Court. The amount in controversy fluctuates depending upon the medical care component of the CPI for all urban consumers. A beneficiary must file a request for review from a judge within 60 days after that person receives notice of the Appeals Council's determination.

Chapter 8: Pros and Cons of Filing Suit

If the external appeal does not result in a reversal of the coverage denial or if the beneficiary decides to skip the external appeal, then the beneficiary also has the choice of filing a lawsuit against the insurer. The upside to a lawsuit is that it puts immediate pressure on the insurer. Many clients fear that if they raise suit against their current insurer, then the insurer will retaliate against them by limiting their coverage or unreasonably denying additional claims. While such retaliation is possible, it would be highly illegal and based on experience, highly unlikely. In contrast, insurance companies that may have ignored members' complaints in the past will usually pay a lot more attention when that member has initiated a legal action. Further, a lawsuit can result in complete coverage for the medical treatment that the client seeks, in addition to the possibility of additional damages for the insurance company's bad faith in denying the claim.

SECTION II: LITIGATING A BAD FAITH ACTION

Chapter 9: Pleading a Bad Faith Case

Pleading a bad faith case requires specific facts sufficient to show the basis for the claim you are advancing. *Davaloo v. State Farm Ins. Co.*, (2005) 135 Cal.App.4th 409 [37 Cal.Rptr.3d 528], emphasized that a plaintiff in a bad-faith action must plead specific facts sufficient to apprise an insurance company of the factual basis of the claim asserted against it. The court determined that the plaintiffs' initial bad-faith complaint was so devoid of factual allegations that plaintiffs' first amended complaint could not relate back to the initial complaint and, as a result, the action was time barred.

In *Davaloo*, the plaintiffs were State Farm policyholders whose properties were damaged in the Northridge earthquake. The opinion involved two coordinated cases filed by the same law firm. California Code of Civil Procedure section 340.9 revived certain time-barred claims against insurers based on claims arising out of the Northridge earthquake. On December 31, 2001, the last day to bring claims under section 340.9, plaintiffs sued State Farm for bad faith and other causes of action arising out of their

Northridge earthquake claims.

Plaintiffs' complaints contained generic allegations based on State Farm's failure to pay benefits for earthquake damage but included no specific allegations of a particular dispute between plaintiffs and State Farm. They alleged that plaintiffs suffered losses in the Northridge earthquake and made timely claims with State Farm. They also made what the court described as generic allegations "describing the full range of improper actions any insurer theoretically could have taken in response to a claim for policy benefits for damages caused by the Northridge earthquake but give no specifics of any kind as to a dispute between the plaintiff(s) specified in the caption and State Farm." The complaints failed to identify the property addresses, the policy numbers or any of the terms of the policies. The complaints also failed to mention CCP § 340.9 and did not refer to the parties by name except in the caption.

More than a year later, plaintiffs filed amended complaints that included more specific factual allegations. State Farm successfully demurred to the amended complaints on the ground that the actions were time-barred because the amended complaints did not relate back to the original complaints because the original complaints were so factually devoid that they were sham complaints.

On appeal, the court reasoned that a complaint must contain a "statement of facts constituting the cause of action, in ordinary and concise language."[2] This fact-pleading requirement compels a plaintiff to allege ultimate facts that "as a whole apprise the defendant of the factual basis of the claim." The court explained that:

> When a complaint complies with the fact-pleading requirement … the existence of a legal right in an abstract form is never alleged by the plaintiff; but,

> instead thereof, the facts from which that right arises are set forth and the right itself is inferred therefrom. The cause of action, as it appears in the complaint when properly pleaded, will therefore always be the facts from which the plaintiff's primary right and the defendant's corresponding primary duty have arisen, together with the *facts* which constitute the defendant's delict or act of wrong."[3]

The court reasoned that an amended complaint relates back to an original complaint if it is based on the same general facts and refers to the same *offending instrumentalities, accident and injuries* as the original complaint. The court ruled that the original complaints were so factually devoid that they did not meet the minimal fact- pleading requirements of section 425.10(a) and were "the functional equivalent of no complaint at all."[4] The court believed that, at bottom, the original complaints alleged nothing more than that the Northridge earthquake caused harm to residents in Los Angeles County. As a result, the allegations failed to apprise State Farm of the factual basis of the claim. There was nothing in the complaints that informed State Farm of the "nature, source and extent" of plaintiff's claims.[5]

The court declined to provide a bright-line rule regarding when a complaint is so factually defective that it fails to meet the minimum fact-pleading requirements of section §425.10(a). It emphasized that it was relying on the "totality of the deficiencies" in the complaints, and not on any single defect or combination of defects.[6]

Although *Davaloo* did not really make new law, plaintiffs must ensure that their complaints include sufficient factual specificity. Wherever possible, plaintiffs should attach their insurance policy (including the policy's declarations page) and all significant correspondence regarding the claim to the complaint. Of course, for strategic reasons, plaintiffs may want to omit certain facts from the complaint (recognizing, of course, that bad facts will eventually become known.)

In order to sufficiently plead a bad faith cause of action, plaintiffs must plead that (1) they are in a contractual relationship with the insurance company or are an express beneficiary of an insurance policy; (2) that benefits are due under the policy; and (3) that the insurance company's withholding of benefits is unreasonable.[7]

But to recover punitive damages, a plaintiff must also plead facts that establish that the insurer's conduct was malicious, oppressive or fraudulent. "The same evidence is relevant both to the finding of bad faith and the imposition of punitive damages, but the conduct required to award punitive damages for the tortuous breach of contract ... is of a different dimension than that required to find bad faith."[8]

Chapter 10: Developing the Case in Discovery

When creating a discovery plan, remember the plaintiffs' burden in the litigation. To win on bad faith and punitive damages, the plaintiff must establish that the insurer's conduct was not only unreasonable, but malicious, oppressive or fraudulent. This means that the plaintiff must prove that the insurer's conduct in withholding benefits was not simply an honest mistake and that the insurer failed to keep its policyholder's interests equal to its own interests. These goals should guide every step taken in the litigation.

Review the insurance policy to evaluate whether the claim was properly denied based on the language of the policy. If there is a coverage question or a dispute concerning the policy interpretation, seek discovery regarding all of the insurer's internal policies, procedures, and guidelines regarding the interpretation of the language at issue. And seek all of the insurer's other documents regarding the interpretation of the language. The insurer may have documents establishing that it was on notice that the language was ambiguous before it denied the claim at issue. Plaintiffs should also obtain all of the past versions of the policy that were in effect before the relevant time period. If the insurer reduced the policy's coverage in the past, evaluate whether it provided sufficient notice of the reduction in coverage for the reduction to become effective. (Insurance Code § 678 governs the requirements for a notice of reductions in coverage.)

Obtain all documents relating to the insurer's adjustment of the claim. These documents are normally contained in the claim file. The claim file documents the insurer's handling of the claim. It should reflect everything that the insurer did to handle the claim. The claim file should identify all of the individuals who worked on the claim, and should detail what investigation they performed, what decisions they made, and the basis for the decisions. Use the claim file to develop a detailed factual chronology of the insurer's handling of the claim.

When reviewing the claim file, evaluate whether the insurer performed a thorough investigation of the claim, whether it objectively evaluated the claim, whether it looked for ways to find coverage, and whether it reasonably handled the claim. Also pay attention to what the insurer failed to do. Often, it helps to think of what a perfect investigation into the claim would have involved and then compare the perfect investigation with the insurer's actual investigation. As an aside, you should almost never settle a bad faith case without reviewing the claim file. If an attorney defending a bad faith claim wants to negotiate settlement before producing the claim file, you can bet that the claim file contains helpful evidence.

Serve a request for production of the underwriting file. The underwriting file should reflect the insurer's activities in connection with the issuance of the policy and can establish what information the insurer knew at the time that it issued the policy. For example, where a property insurer rescinded a policy on the ground that the application failed to disclose that the property had a swimming pool, the insurer's rescission was undermined by the fact that its underwriting file contained a picture of the property that showed the swimming pool. Also obtain a copy of the application for insurance.

Seek discovery of all of the insurer's policies, procedures and guidelines regarding claims handling. Evaluate whether the insurer's handling of the claim at issue complied with its own guidelines. Its failure to do so can be strong evidence of bad faith. If it did adhere to its guidelines, but in doing so it nevertheless acted unreasonably, there could be evidence of systemic bad faith.

Ask for and examine the documents that the insurer used to train its adjusters to handle claims. These documents can help establish that the insurer systemically fails to train its adjusters to handle claims properly. Insurers often do not maintain these documents. If not, their absence may support an inference that there was no training, or that the materials contained information that the insurer did not want to become public.

Because strong trial themes in bad-faith cases include promises and lies, propound document requests for all of the insurer's advertising documents. These documents can be used to create a chart that compares the promises that the insurer made when it sold the policy to the insurer's actual conduct in handling the claim. All too often, the insurer's marketing department and its claims department seem to have never met.

In California, plaintiffs should also serve form interrogatories that define "incident" as the circumstances and events surrounding the insurer's investigation into the claim and denial of the claim at issue. Plaintiffs should check the boxes under the headings 3, 4, 6-9, 12, 13, 15.1, 17.1 (if requests for admission are also served), and 50. Plaintiffs should serve special interrogatories that ask the insurer to identify all policy provisions and facts that it used to deny the claim, all individuals involved in the handling of the claim, and all files that exist relating to the claim.

After obtaining all of the relevant documents, plaintiffs should depose the important adjusters involved in the handling of the claim. It is often helpful to first depose the insurer's "person most knowledgeable" about the handling of the claim. If the witness does not appear knowledgeable about the claim, it opens the door at trial to the argument that person the company claimed knew more about the claim than anyone else actually knows little. This reflects poorly on the carrier. During the adjusters' depositions, review the training they received regarding claims handling and pin down exactly what they did to handle the claim. Ask whether they handled the claim consistently with the way that the company had instructed them to.

Plaintiffs should carefully consider whether to retain insurance experts to testify as expert witnesses regarding insurance industry practices and the insurer's handling of the claim. In *Neal v. Farmers Ins. Exch.* (1978) 21 Cal.3d 910, 924 [148 Cal.Rptr. 389, 396], the court suggested that expert witnesses can be helpful in bad faith cases. But many bad faith experts agree that if you need an expert to prove your bad faith case, you are in trouble. The type of bad faith that will make a jury angry enough to award punitive damages is usually apparent from the record alone, without an expert to explain to the jury why the conduct was unreasonable.

Chapter 11: Developing Pattern and Practice Evidence

Insurance companies frequently deny claims as a result of company-wide policies or practices that affect many policyholders. In order to determine whether an insurer's conduct towards your client is part of a pattern and practice of similar behavior towards other policyholders, it is crucial to serve *pattern and practice* discovery. Plaintiffs in bad faith cases should conduct extensive discovery into an insurer's business practices to understand how a plaintiff's claim fits into the larger context of an insurer's pattern and practice of unfair claims handling. Developing evidence of a pattern and practice of unfair claims handling will help establish that the insurer acted in bad faith and that the plaintiff's harm resulted from the insurer's intentional malice, trickery or deceit and not simply from an accident.

Plaintiffs often assert causes of action for unfair business practices alleging that the insurer is engaging in a pattern and practice of improper conduct. Policyholders can still state a cause of action against insurers for unfair, unlawful or fraudulent conduct in handling claims under California Business and Professions Code section 17200.[9]

Plaintiffs should seek discovery regarding similar claims from policyholders, complaints to the insurer about similar issues, and other litigation against the company. Plaintiffs should also network with other counsel litigating similar actions against the company and use the other actions to develop pattern and practice evidence.

Insurers generally object to pattern and practice discovery on the ground that producing the information would be burdensome and oppressive. They routinely submit declarations indicating that it will cost hundreds of thousands of dollars to produce the information. For example, in *Mead Reinsurance Co. v. Sup. Ct. (City of Laguna Beach)* (1986) 188 Cal.App.3d 313, 317 [232 Cal.Rptr 752, 754], the court found pattern and practice discovery burdensome and oppressive where it would require production of over 13,000 claim files without allocating the costs of producing the files.

To preempt this problem, before serving discovery, depose the insurer's custodian of records and person most knowledgeable regarding information technologies to determine how the insurer maintains its files and data. You can then craft your discovery requests to minimize the burden on the insurer.

Insurers also object on the ground that the discovery would violate policyholders' right to privacy under Insurance Code section 791.01 and/or the Constitutional right to privacy. When you serve your discovery, you should send the insurer a form letter that it can send to its insureds to obtain their consent to produce their information. The letter should include a brief description of the bad faith allegations and explain that the insureds' records may be relevant to the case. If relevant, also include a description of any unfair business practice allegations. If insureds understand that they may be a victim of the insurer's bad faith or unfair business practices, they will be more likely to release their records. Importantly, the policyholder must date and sign the letter within one year of the production of the information. Alternately, at the time you propound document discovery, offer that all personally identifying information can be redacted from produced documents. Then, if the produced documents support a claim that your client was injured by a pattern and practice of unreasonable or illegal claims handling practices, you can request that a letter be sent to the insureds to obtain their consent to unredacted versions of the documents and/or their contact information.

If the insurer resists and a motion is necessary, you can explain to the court that not only is the discovery sought relevant as substantive evidence to prove the truth of plaintiff's claims, but is also relevant because these third party insureds are actually potential witnesses to this case. Since those third party insureds are victims of the same unlawful behavior at issue in your case, they could potentially testify as to defendants' pattern and practice of claims handling. The discovery sought by the letter to third party insureds would allow people whose cases are directly relevant to this case an opportunity to contribute to evidence supporting the argument that the insurer engages in a pattern and practice of this unreasonable and/or unlawful behavior. Notably, in *Pioneer Electrics (USA), Inc. v. Superior Court* (2007) 40 Cal.4th 360 (53 Cal. Rptr. 3d 513), which was decided after *Colonial Life*, the Supreme Court found that disclosure of such person's contact information is directly contemplated by the discovery statutes because these persons qualify as "percipient witnesses" to defendants' pattern and practice conduct. The Court also weighed the competing interests in a discovering third-parties' contact information and their rights to privacy. Specifically, the Supreme Court considered "the extent to which California's right to privacy provision (Cal. Const., art. I, § 1) protects [] purchasers from having their identifying information disclosed to the plaintiff during civil discovery proceedings in a consumers' rights class action against the seller." It held:

> [W]e think the trial court properly evaluated the alternatives, balanced the competing interests, and permitted disclosure of contact information regarding Pioneer's complaining customers unless, following proper notice to them, they registered a written objection. These customers had no reasonable expectation of any greater degree of privacy, and no serious invasion of their privacy interests would be threatened by requiring them affirmatively to object to disclosure.

Finally, in all trials jurors want to know why the parties acted the way that they did. If you can establish that the insurer engaged in the bad faith conduct towards your client because of a systemic practice that damages other policyholders, the jurors will be more likely to punish the insurer to deter similar conduct in the future.

Insurance companies frequently deny claims as a result of company-wide policies or practices that affect many policyholders. Under California bad faith law, evidence demonstrating that the defendant insurance company has engaged in a widespread illegal practice or a practice that has been harmful to its insureds is directly relevant to not only proving bad faith, but also to establishing liability on punitive damages claims. In order to determine whether an insurer's conduct towards your client is part of a pattern and practice of similar behavior towards other policyholders, it is crucial to serve *pattern and practice* discovery.

Chapter 12: *Colonial Life* and Pattern and Practice Evidence

California law has long recognized that similar acts of misconduct are relevant in insurance bad faith actions. (*Colonial Life & Accident Ins. Co. v. Superior Court* (1982) 31 Cal.3d 785 [183 Cal.Rptr. 810].) In *Colonial Life*, the plaintiff brought a third-party bad faith action arising out of Colonial Life's unreasonable refusal to settle her claim. Plaintiff had been injured and developed progressive gangrene that caused doctors to amputate her leg. Colonial Life employed a claims-adjusting company, Equifax, to adjust the claim. Equifax employed a claims adjuster, Sharkey. Colonial Life, through Equifax and Sharkey, claimed that the policy did not cover plaintiff's leg amputation, refused to tender the policy limits, and made a low settlement offer.

Plaintiff served Equifax with a request to produce all documents relating to claims that Sharkey handled for Equifax. Equifax objected that the request sought irrelevant documents and invaded the other policyholders' rights of privacy under California Insurance Code section 791.01. The trial court ordered Equifax to produce the names and addresses of the Colonial Life claimants.

Colonial Life filed a writ of mandate to stop plaintiff's counsel from obtaining the names and records of the claimants on the ground that the information was not relevant. The California Supreme Court rejected Colonial Life's argument as "patently meritless." It reasoned that Insurance Code section 790.03(h) precludes insurers from "knowingly committing or performing with such frequency as to indicate a general business practice a variety of unfair claim settlement practices." Plaintiff may establish a bad faith claim by showing that the acts that harmed him were knowingly committed or engaged in with such frequency as to indicate a general business practice. And plaintiff can prove that an insurer knowingly committed such acts through circumstantial evidence. Thus, discovery addressing the "frequency of alleged unfair settlement practices" is likely to produce relevant evidence.

The Court also reasoned that other instances of unfair settlement practices may be highly relevant to plaintiff's punitive damages claim. In California, to be liable for punitive damages, a defendant must act with the intent to vex, injure or annoy or with a conscious disregard for a plaintiff's rights. A plaintiff may prove these elements directly or by implication. And a plaintiff can prove these elements through indirect evidence of a pattern of unfair practices.

The Court cited *Neal v. Farmers Ins. Exchange* (1978) 21 Cal.3d 910, 922 [148 Cal.Rptr. 389] for the proposition that it previously affirmed a punitive damages award based on an insurer's failure to settle where the evidence showed that the failure to settle was part of a "conscious course of conduct, firmly grounded in established company policy." The Court also noted that the evidence may be relevant to prove ratification by Colonial Life for punitive damages.

To protect the policyholders' rights of privacy, the Court required plaintiff's counsel to send a letter to the other claimants to obtain their consent to release their records.

Chapter 13: The Legacy of *Colonial Life*

Similar to the plaintiff in *Colonial Life*, in *Moore v. American United Life Insurance Company* (1984) 150 Cal.App.3d 610 [197 Cal.Rptr. 878], plaintiff sued her disability insurer for wrongfully denying her claim. The definition of "total disability" in plaintiff's policy was narrower than the relevant definition of "total disability" for *any occupation* disability policies under California law. Plaintiff claimed that American United engaged in a pattern and practice of obtaining misleading opinions from physicians by providing them with a definition of "total disability" that was narrower than the applicable definition under California law. Plaintiff also alleged that American United routinely misled its policyholders by including the narrower definition of total disability in their policies. Plaintiff contended that American United knew before it denied plaintiff's claim that its definition of total disability did not comply with California law.

Plaintiff introduced evidence at trial regarding two other American United disability claims to establish American United's pattern and practice of improper claims handling and to show that American United knew that its definition of "total disability" was improper under California law.

The jury awarded plaintiff $30,000 for compensatory damages and $2.5 million in punitive damages. American United appealed on the ground that evidence regarding the other claims was not relevant to any disputed fact. Relying on *Colonial Life*, the Court found that the evidence was relevant to establishing a pattern and practice of unreasonable claims handling. American United also argued that evidence regarding the other claim was not relevant because it was not factually similar to plaintiff's claim as it involved a different definition of total disability. The Court rejected the argument and found that the policies were substantially similar. Finally, the Court rejected American United's argument that the danger of undue prejudice substantially outweighed any probative value of the evidence.

American United also argued that the jury's punitive damages award was excessive. In upholding the award, the court evaluated the reprehensibility of American United's conduct. It reasoned that the plaintiff presented evidence of "fraudulent claims practices potentially affecting numerous insureds other than the plaintiff." The punitive damages award punished American United for engaging in a pattern and practice firmly grounded in established company policy that had the potential of defrauding numerous insureds other than the plaintiff. The Court noted:

> The jury could conclude that defendant consciously pursued a practice or policy of cheating insureds out of benefits by obtaining incorrect opinions of total disability from treating physicians.[10]

Mock v. Michigan Millers: *Colonial Life* discovery and punitive damages

In *Mock v. Michigan Millers Mut. Ins. Co.* (1992) 4

Cal.App.4th 306 [5 Cal.Rtpr.2d 594], the court emphasized that pattern and practice evidence is relevant to establishing punitive damages against an insurer. The court surveyed cases affirming an award of punitive damages again an insurer and noted that an established pattern and practice of bad faith was a common element. Specifically, the court explained:

> [A] central theme common to those cases which have sustained punitive awards is the existence of *established policies or practices* in claims handling which are harmful to insureds. (See. e.g., *Moore v. American United Life Ins. Co.* (1984) 150 Cal.App.3rd 610, 637 [197 Cal.Rptr. 878] [insurer had a practice 'firmly grounded in established company policy' of intentionally supplying physicians with the wrong definition of total disability]; *Downey Savings & Loan Ass'n. v. Ohio Casualty Ins. Co.* (1987) 189 Cal.App.3rd 1072, 1098-1099 [234 Cal.Rptr. 835] [insurer was guilty of company-wide misconduct by instructing its claims adjusters to focus on ways to defeat claims]; *Hughes v. Blue Cross of Northern California* (1989) 215 Cal.App.3rd 832, 847 [263 Cal.Rptr. 850] [insurer's objectionable claims handling practices were rooted in *established* company practice]; *Liberty Transport Inc. v. Harry W. Gorst Co.* supra, 229 Cal.App.3rd 417, 436-437 [280 Cal.Rtpr. 159] [insurer had a *company policy* of never communicating directly with their insureds and despite knowledge of insured's ignorance of decision to deny claim did nothing to correct the error].) In *Patrick v. Maryland Casualty Co.*, supra., the court seemed to suggest that what was required was a 'consistent and unremedied pattern of egregious insurer practices.' (217 Cal.App.3rd at 1576 [267 Cal.Rptr. 24.]) (Emphasis in text.)

TXO Production v. Alliance Resources: The use of pattern and practice outside of bad faith

The United States Supreme Court's decision in *TXO Production Corp. v. Alliance Resources Corp.* (1993) 509 U.S. 443, 460-461 [113 S.Ct. 2711], provides an example of one way to obtain pattern and practice evidence. Although not an insurance bad faith case, the court affirmed a punitive damage award in part because "TXO's pattern of behavior could potentially cause millions of dollars in damages to other victims." The court concluded that although the punitive damages award was large, "in light of … the bad faith of petitioner, *the fact that the scheme employed in this case was part of a larger pattern of fraud, trickery and deceit*, and petitioner's wealth, we are not persuaded that the award was" grossly excessive.[11]

The Supreme Court decision does not explain what evidence in the record supported these statements about the defendant's "larger pattern" of misconduct. However, that evidence is detailed in the decision of the West Virginia Supreme Court, in *TXO Production Corp. v. Alliance Resources Corp.* (1992) 187 W. Va. 457 [419 S.E.2d 870]. In that opinion, the court explains that the plaintiff's "pattern and practice" evidence consisted of the videotaped deposition testimony from four attorneys who had represented other oil producers who had dealt with the defendant and had been forced to file suit to obtain the royalties they thought they were owed.

Specifically, the plaintiff in *TXO* accused the defendant of knowingly recording a false deed to create a cloud on plaintiff's title to oil and gas wells and using that cloud as a basis to reduce the royalty payments *TXO* had agreed to pay for the production on those wells. One of TXO's affirmative defenses at trial was good faith and lack of malice. To rebut this defense, the plaintiff introduced the testimony by the four attorneys to establish a lack of good faith.

The first attorney who testified represented an elderly, functionally illiterate woman in Louisiana. TXO's employees had visited his client and tricked her into signing a lease by telling her that unless she signed "some papers," TXO could not continue to pay her neighbors royalties for gas. They also told her that she did not need to speak to her attorney about their visit. TXO settled the suit.[12] The second attorney testified that he owned oil wells in Texas and TXO had refused for over a year to pay him any royalties on the production from the wells, citing various excuses, including purported uncertainties about the title. TXO ultimately agreed to pay.[13] The third attorney testified that he represented a group of well owners in a suit against TXO for its refusal to pay royalties, which TXO ultimately settled.[14] The fourth lawyer testified about ongoing litigation against TXO in Oklahoma. The suit alleged that TXO misrepresented to a group of landowners that it had the right to drill on their land. As a result, one landowner gave TXO permission to drill on his land, which TXO used to gain the right to drill under the entire tract. In essence, it was able to bootstrap its lie about its right to drill into permission to drill.[15]

The West Virginia Supreme Court found that this evidence was sufficient to disprove TXO's defense of good faith, "and to show that this case was but part of a pattern and practice of deception and chiseling by TXO."[16] The court also found that this hearsay testimony was admissible under the "catchall" hearsay exceptions of the West Virginia Rules of Evidence, (which parallel the Federal Rules of Evidence.) Since TXO was represented by counsel in each deposition, and since it knew well in advance that plaintiff would be seeking to admit the deposition testimony, it had every opportunity to rebut or discredit the testimony. Hence, the testimony was deemed sufficiently credible and reliable to be admitted in evidence.[17]

Chapter 14: The Importance of *Colonial Life* Discovery

Following *State Farm Mut. Auto. Ins. Co. v. Campbell, et al.* (2003) 538 U.S. 408 [123 S.Ct. 1513], pattern and practice evidence is important in obtaining and keeping punitive damage awards. In *Campbell*, State Farm's insured, Campbell, was driving on a two-lane highway and attempted to pass six vans. Ospital was driving in the opposite direction. Ospital swerved to avoid Campbell and crashed into an automobile driven by Slusher. The accident killed Ospital and disabled Slusher. Ospital's successors and Slusher (collectively "accident victims") filed a tort and wrongful death action against Campbell and his wife. Although investigators determined that Campbell caused the crash, State Farm contested liability. State Farm then refused the accident victims' offer to settle the case for the $50,000 policy limit and took the case to trial. State Farm assured the Campbells that Campbell did not cause the accident, that the Campbells' assets were safe, and that the Campbells did not need separate counsel.

The jury determined that Campbell caused the accident and a judgment was entered for roughly $185,000. State

Farm initially refused to cover the $135,000 liability above the $50,000 policy limit, and State Farm refused to post a bond to allow Campbell to appeal the judgment. While the case was on appeal, the Campbells settled with the accident victims. In exchange for the accident victims' agreement to not satisfy their judgment against the Campbells, the Campbells agreed to file a bad faith action against State Farm and assign 90% of any recovery to the accident victims. After the Campbells lost the appeal, State Farm paid the entire judgment.

The Campbells then filed a bad faith action against State Farm. At trial, the jury determined that State Farm's refusal to settle was unreasonable as there was a substantial likelihood of an excess verdict against the Campbells. The Campbells introduced evidence that State Farm took their case to trial as a result of a nation-wide scheme to limit claims payments. The scheme involved State Farm's conduct in numerous states for more than 20 years. State Farm moved to exclude the evidence, but the trial court admitted the evidence on the ground that it was relevant to whether State Farm's conduct was sufficiently egregious to justify punitive damages.

The United States Supreme Court reaffirmed that the degree of *reprehensibility* of an insurer's conduct is the most crucial factor in evaluating a punitive damages award against an insurer. To consider reprehensibility, a court must consider factors, including whether the conduct involved repeated actions or was an isolated incident, and whether the harm was the result of intentional malice, trickery, deceit or simply an accident. Repeated misconduct is more reprehensible than a single instance of misconduct as "a recidivist may be punished more severely than a first offender."

The Supreme Court emphasized that although "evidence of other acts [towards other insureds] need not be identical to have relevance in the calculation of punitive damages," it must have some nexus to plaintiffs' claims. In *Campbell*, instead of focusing on the type of conduct that damaged the Campbells, the Campbells introduced irrelevant evidence that bore no relation to their claim. For example, the Campbells introduced evidence that State Farm's policies generally corrupted its employees and that State Farm had investigated the personal life of one of its employees. This evidence was not relevant in the *Campbell* case and had no nexus to the Campbells' claim. The Court found that the Campbells used the case as a "platform to expose, and punish, the perceived deficiencies of State Farm's operations throughout the country" and that they introduced substantial "evidence pertaining to claims that had nothing to do with a third-party lawsuit." The Court indicated that a "defendant's dissimilar acts, independent from the acts upon which liability was premised," may not serve as the basis for punitive damages. The Campbells failed to show *any* conduct by State Farm that was similar to the conduct that damaged them. As a result, in reducing the punitive damages award, the Supreme Court only considered State Farm's conduct towards the Campbells and did not consider State Farm's conduct towards any other insureds.

In the 2005 *Johnson v. Ford Motor Co.* case, the Supreme Court of California clarified the law further, by explaining that although *State Farm* requires reasonable proportionality between punitive damages and actual or potential harm to the plaintiff, what is a reasonable ratio necessarily depends on the reprehensibility of the conduct, "the most important indicium of the reasonableness award," which, in turn, is influenced by the frequency and profitability of the defendant's prior or contemporaneous similar conduct. In *Johnson v. Ford Motor Co.*, the plaintiffs purchased a used Taurus from a Ford dealership. When asked about the previous ownership, the plaintiffs were told that the Taurus had been traded in for a newer model. When asked to see the car's repair history, they were shown a computer print-out that indicated that there had been no significant repairs. In reality, the Taurus had suffered from repeated and serious transmission problems and the prior owner had requested that Ford repurchase the car as a "lemon." After the plaintiffs experienced repeated transmission problems, Ford replaced the transmission twice and, when plaintiffs again asked to see the car's repair history, they were finally shown the car's complete history, detailing the transmission problems experienced by the first owners.

Plaintiffs sued Ford for, among other things, intentional and negligent misrepresentation, violation of the California Consumer Legal Remedies Act, and violation of California Bus. & Prof. Code section 17500's prohibition on false or misleading advertising. At trial, the plaintiffs introduced evidence that, in order to avoid the title branding and additional requirements involved in reselling a "lemon" automobile under California law, Ford managers employed a narrow concept of what constituted a repair attempt for purposes of applying the state lemon laws. In addition, when customers asked Ford to buy back their vehicles as lemons, Ford would instead offer them "owner appreciation certificates" ("OACs") that acted as credits on trade-ins for new Ford vehicles. This not only avoided having to brand the repurchased vehicles as "lemons," but also saved Ford thousands of dollars for each transaction. Plaintiffs presented further evidence that Ford's San Francisco and Los Angeles offices issued about 1,200 to 1,400 OACs per year in the year of trial and the previous year (2000 and 2001). The average face amount of OACs issued over the four previous years was between $2,700 and $3,200. Finally, testimony was given to the effect that the cost of reacquiring a vehicle as a lemon (i.e., the cost of repurchasing or replacing the vehicle less its resale or salvage value) was between $8,500 and $13,500, depending on the year and the method of reacquisition (refund or replacement).

Based on this evidence, the plaintiffs' attorney argued to the jury that Ford saved $6,000 to $10,000 on each OAC for a vehicle that would otherwise have had to be reacquired, and that approximately 1,000 such OACs were issued per year to California customers (excluding some issued out of California offices to customers in other states). Counsel estimated Ford's savings in California from "this whole scheme of owner appreciation certificates"—that is, the practice of issuing OACs for vehicles that should have been reacquired as lemons, and of failing to provide warranty buyback notices on all vehicles traded in with OACs, thus concealing the vehicles' defects from subsequent buyers—to be $6 to $10 million per year for 2000 and 2001. He urged the jury, in order to deter Ford from continuing that conduct, to impose punitive damages in an amount that would, at least, take from Ford all those wrongful profits.

The jury found in plaintiffs' favor and awarded them $17,811.60 in compensatory damages, and 10 million in punitive damages. The Court of Appeal, holding Ford could constitutionally be punished only for its fraud on plaintiffs and not for its overall course of conduct, reduced the punitive damages award to $53,435, approximately three times the compensatory damages.

The Supreme Court reversed. The Supreme Court's decision was based on its holding that, although the Court of Appeal correctly rejected the aggregate disgorgement approach (because, among other things, it created an end-around the requirements of the class action device by awarding damages based on profits earned from transactions with a large class of similar claimants without ever having to prove the specifics of those "hypothetical claims"), it did not properly consider the evidence of Ford's policies and practices, and their scale and profitability, in analyzing the reprehensibility of Ford's conduct. According to the Supreme Court, a reasonable ratio necessarily depends on the reprehensibility of the conduct which is influenced by the frequency and profitability of the defendant's prior or contemporaneous similar conduct.

Chapter 15: The California Supreme Court's Decision Not to Limit *Colonial Life*

The case of *Permanent General Assurance Co., v. Sup. Ct.*, which the California Supreme Court depublished (previously published at (2004) 122 Cal.App.4th 1493 [19 Cal.Rptr.3d 597]), could have narrowed the scope of permissible pattern and practice evidence. In the case, a policyholder sued her insurer for bad faith and other causes of action after the insurer denied her claim arising out of the theft of her automobile. She sought the production of all of the insurer's claim files relating to automobile thefts since 1998. She argued that the insurer was engaging in racially discriminatory claims handling practices and that the claim files were relevant to her bad faith claim. The insurer objected on the grounds that the request was burdensome, overbroad, harassing, irrelevant and sought private information protected by Insurance Code section 791. Strangely, the insurer also claimed that under *Campbell*, pattern and practice evidence was irrelevant to plaintiff's punitive damages claim. The trial court granted plaintiff's motion to compel the discovery and did not require the other policyholders to sign consent forms to release their claim files.

Division Three of the Fourth Appellate District ultimately agreed that the pattern and practice discovery should be produced, but conditioned the production on obtaining the policyholders' consent to release their records. The court addressed plaintiff's four arguments regarding why the discovery was relevant.

First, the court determined that *Colonial Life* did not compel the production of the claim files. The court poorly distinguished *Colonial Life* on the ground that it was a third-party bad faith case and that the law no longer recognizes third-party bad faith. Second, the court rejected plaintiff's argument that the discovery was relevant to a potential unfair business practices claim essentially because the law no longer recognizes third-party bad faith. Third, the court rejected plaintiff's argument that the discovery was relevant to establish punitive damages under *Campbell.* It found that the potential for punitive damages did not justify the pattern and practice discovery.

Finally, the court ordered production of the claim files because they were relevant to plaintiff's theory that the insurer had a practice of racially discriminatory claims handling. The logic seemed somewhat tortured in that the pattern and practice discovery was relevant to show racially discriminatory claims handling but not other types of systemic bad faith claims handling (like unreasonably denying or delaying claims). Ultimately, the California Supreme Court could have taken the case and modified the scope of permissible pattern and practice evidence. But it simply depublished the case.

Chapter 16: Guide Your Case through Summary Judgment by Focused Discovery and Pleading

A motion for summary judgment and/or adjudication is one of the most important—if not *the* most important—motion that can be made during litigation. Therefore, preparation for either making or opposing a motion for summary judgment should begin early, ideally right after a complaint is filed.

Understanding the Summary Judgment Timeline

A motion for summary judgment/adjudication has a 75-day notice period, and it must be heard at least 30 days before trial. The normal time for responding to most discovery requests (*e.g.*, interrogatories, requests for admission, document demands) is a minimum of 30 days. Thus, discovery will have to be served early—at least 8-9 months before trial—to ensure that you have all needed information to either bring or oppose a motion for summary judgment/adjudication. Requests for an extension of time to respond to discovery are common and generally granted, and motions to compel discovery are often necessary to obtain supplemental responses on disputed discovery. Also, if your case involves substantial electronically-stored information, you will need the extra amount of time to resolve issues regarding the scope of the search and manner of production. Although depositions have a short notice period, just 10 days if the deposition notice is served by hand or 15 days if it is served by mail – in order to effectively take a deposition, you should have all relevant documents prior to the deposition so that you can ask the witness about them and, if appropriate, have the witness authenticate the documents and establish any hearsay exceptions that may be applicable. Therefore, ideally, document discovery should be completed, or at least be well underway, at the time depositions are noticed. Although requests for production can also be served with notices of deposition, a responding party can object and show up at the deposition without the requested documents so it is usually a better strategy to try to obtain the documents through earlier document demands.

Lastly, it is important to keep in mind that absent circumstances beyond your control, the court is not likely to grant a continuance of the trial date merely to give you more time to obtain needed discovery on a motion for summary judgment.

The Pleadings Frame the Issues for Motions for Summary Judgment/Adjudication

A summary judgment motion must show that the "material facts" are undisputed.[18] The pleadings, *i.e.*, the complaint and answer, serve as the outer measure of materiality in a summary judgment motion, and the motion may not be granted or denied on issues not raised by the pleadings. Therefore, study the claims asserted in the complaint and the affirmative defenses made in the answer to determine what facts will be at issue in the case and possibly challenged on a motion for summary judgment/adjudication. If you are not sure what the elements are of a particular claim or affirmative defense, and, therefore, what facts will be at issue in your case, you can use "CACI" (California Civil Jury Instructions) or "BAJI" (Book of Approved Jury Instructions) as a checklist of the substantive law involved in your case. These instructions indicate the elements that a plaintiff must prove at trial to recover and the elements that a defendant must prove to prevail on an affirmative defense. The Pleadings chapter in Witkin, California Procedure, also has a table of contents that can be used as a checklist for the elements of each claim or affirmative defense.

Useful Discovery in Preparation for Making or Opposing a Motion for Summary Judgment

If you will be bringing a motion for summary judgment/adjudication, you will need to take discovery aimed at establishing "undisputed" material facts. If you anticipate opposing a motion for summary judgment, the opposite is true and you will need to obtain information through discovery establishing that there are disputed material facts. In either situation, the same types of discovery procedures can be used.

The official Judicial Council form interrogatories are very useful for marshalling the evidence either in support of or in opposition to a motion for summary judgment/adjudication. The questions in the "50" series of the official form interrogatories are useful for obtaining facts where a case involves an alleged breach of contract. For instance, they can be used to determine whether a defendant claims that the contract was unenforceable or that performance under the contract was excused. Those questions in the "12" series are good for identifying witnesses with pertinent knowledge and identifying any reports, film or videotapes containing relevant information. For plaintiffs, form interrogatory 15.1 should always be propounded after the answer is filed to obtain the facts upon which a defendant will rely in support of its affirmative defenses and 16.1 is also important for obtaining information regarding a defendant's contentions as to the plaintiff's alleged damages.

Requests for admissions ("RFAs") are another very useful tool for marshalling the evidence to bring or oppose a motion for summary judgment. RFAs may be used as to any matter within the permissible scope of discovery: *i.e.*, "relevant to the subject matter of the action" and not otherwise privileged or protected from discovery. RFAs are commonly used to establish the genuineness or authenticity of specified documents. RFAs can also be used to establish the truth of specified facts, and to ask an opponent to admit the truth of legal conclusions. As for the latter, for instance, RFAs can be propounded asking whether specified acts were "negligent," whether such negligence was the "legal cause" of the plaintiff's injuries, or whether a third person was an "authorized agent" or was acting in the "course and scope of employment." RFAs can also be used as the foundation for a motion for summary adjudication on a defendant's affirmative defenses. If the defendant's admissions show that it has no evidence on a particular element of a defense, then that may satisfy your burden of proof on a summary judgment motion to show no triable issue of fact. Form interrogatory 17.1 should always be propounded with requests for admissions to obtain the facts supporting a defendant's denial of an RFA.

Document demands should be propounded asking for all documents identified in response to form interrogatories, all documents regarding the plaintiff, and any other documents that may have relevant information. To the extent not covered by form interrogatories, special interrogatories should be propounded to obtain the name of all witnesses who have information supporting the defendants' affirmative defenses and general denial, all facts supporting such affirmative defenses and general denial, and to ask the defendant to identify all documents supporting its affirmative defenses.

Once you have gathered the relevant documents, then you should depose the witnesses with personal knowledge of facts essential to the plaintiff's claims and the defendant's affirmative defenses and general denial. Admissions made in deposition are particularly important on a motion for summary judgment because they govern and control any contradictory declaration submitted by the witness in connection with a motion for summary judgment. Such witnesses should also be questioned about any documents they drafted, received, or otherwise may have had any involvement with or seen before. These witnesses' testimony can be used to establish the authenticity of such documents and any exceptions to the hearsay rule that may be applicable, *e.g.*, the business records exception and the party admission exception. The latter is particularly important since the same evidentiary rules that govern admissibility of documents at trial also apply on a motion for summary judgment. In other words, all documentary evidence presented on a motion for summary judgment must be admissible: it must be properly identified and authenticated; admissible under the secondary evidence rule, *i.e.*, a true and correct copy of the original; and either nonhearsay or admissible under some exception to the hearsay rule.

Although expert discovery often happens after motions for summary judgment are briefed, a plaintiff may often find it useful or even necessary to submit an expert's declaration in connection with a motion for summary judgment. Declarations by expert witnesses are required when expert witness testimony would be required at trial, *e.g.*, the standard of care in a professional malpractice case. The requirements for admissibility of an expert's declaration on a motion for summary judgment are the same as if the expert were testifying at trial. The Evidence Code restricts expert testimony to opinions based on a "matter ... perceived by or personally known to the witness" when that matter "is of a type that reasonably may be relied upon by an expert in forming an opinion ... (A)n expert opinion based on speculation or conjecture is inadmissible." The declaration must contain facts showing the expert's qualifications (competency) to express the opinion in question, *e.g.*, facts showing the expert has the training, experience or necessary skill to render an opinion on the particular matters in controversy.

Lastly, another source of evidence to support or oppose a motion for summary judgment is admissions previously made by the opposing party. Admissions of material facts made in an opposing party's pleadings are binding on that party as "judicial admissions." They are conclusive concessions of the truth of those matters, are effectively removed as issues from the litigation, and may not be contradicted by the party whose pleadings are used against him or her. Therefore, judicial admissions can be used to establish an undisputed fact on a motion for summary judgment. Admissions obtained through discovery, either by way of deposition testimony (as mentioned above), responses to interrogatories, or responses to RFAs, will also bind an opposing party and controverting declarations will be disregarded.

SECTION III: PRE-TRIAL AND TRIAL

One of the most important steps in preparing for trial is building evidence grids. An evidence grid is a chart listing the elements of a cause of action or affirmative defense and the evidence that will support each element. Creating evidence grids forces you to critically examine what evidence you can use to establish each element of your case and strategize about the admissibility of each item of evidence. Moreover, it will enable you to intelligently structure the order of your witnesses to maximize the impact of your case on the jury. Draft evidence grids for each cause of action and affirmative defense in your case.

Chapter 17: Developing Themes

The trial of a bad faith case is about competing stories. The policyholder's attorney and the insurer's attorney present different stories to explain the facts of the case. Developing themes is an essential component of storytelling. Themes will provide a context through which the jurors can view and understand the case.

The most prevalent themes in bad faith cases include *promises and broken promises.* The policyholder believed the insurer's promises, faithfully paid his premiums, and then the insurer broke its promises to the policyholder in their time of need. Buying insurance is very different than buying other products. When people purchase a cup of coffee at Starbucks, they can smell it, taste it and drink it. When people buy a car they can immediately drive it. In contrast, people cannot test drive an insurance policy. Most people buy insurance with the hope that they will never need to use their insurance policy. They purchase health insurance with the hope that they will remain healthy and never need to rely on their health insurance. People purchase homeowners insurance with the hope that their home will not burn down. They purchase insurance to buy peace of mind. People rely on "the good hands people" and the company that "gets you back where you belong."

After believing their insurer, did the insurer honor its obligations? In the policyholder's time of need did the insurer work for the policyholder to protect their interests or did it work against the policyholder? Did the insurer look for ways to find coverage and keep the policyholder's interests equal to the insurer's interests? Or did it take a myopic view of the claim and focus only on ways to deny the claim?

In addition, corporate greed is a common policyholder theme. Where policyholders can show that an insurer engaged in a pattern and practice of unreasonable conduct towards its claimants, jurors are more likely to find bad faith and award punitive damages. For example, in the context of homeowners' insurance, where policyholders can establish that an insurer systemically instructed its adjusters to low ball claims, the jurors will be more likely to enter a large bad faith award.

Along with corporate greed, bad faith cases often include a theme of *David v. Goliath.* Human nature favors the underdog. Where the policyholder is an individual or a small business, jurors generally feel more affinity with the policyholder than a large insurance company. This becomes more pronounced when the insurer has a team of defense attorneys in the courtroom and the policyholder is represented by a single attorney.

Although these themes are generally powerful in most bad faith cases, in each case the themes must be tested in focus groups. Focus groups are an invaluable way to explore whether your themes are effective or whether they should be revised or abandoned.

Chapter 18: Voir Dire

There are a million different opinions on how attorneys should conduct voir dire but rarely do lawyers discuss what conduct is actually allowed during voir dire. This chapter briefly reviews what voir dire is and the basic rules that govern voir dire in California's state civil courts.

Voir dire is French for "to speak the truth," but legal jurists in America use it to describe a "preliminary examination of a prospective juror by a judge or lawyer to decide whether the prospect is qualified and suitable to serve on a jury."[19] In other words, voir dire constitutes the jury-selection phase of a trial. Voir dire is the trial attorney's chance to gain insight into the minds of potential jurors and to exercise disqualifications of potential jurors where warranted. The process begins with a jury commissioner who estimates the number of prospective jurors that may be required to serve the needs of the court, and issues summons to prospective jurors for service.[20] The jury commissioner then randomly sends some of these prospective jurors to specific courts to form a jury panel.[21] From this group, a jury, of at most 12 persons but can be less should the parties agree to it, is formed.[22] Once the prospective jurors arrive at a court room, the court room's clerk randomly selects the names of the jurors for voir dire until the entire jury is selected or the panel is exhausted.[23]

Voir dire begins with an opportunity for the judge to examine the prospective jurors. [24] The California Code of Civil Procedure then provides a right to each party to have their counsel examine with direct questioning any of the prospective jurors "in order to enable counsel to intelligently exercise both peremptory challenges and challenges for cause."[25] This scheme is significantly different from that in federal courts where the trial judge has complete discretion as to how to conduct voir dire and whether to allow the parties' counsel a chance to conduct their own examination at all. [26] The parties do not have the codified rights that those in California state courts have concerning voir dire.[27] In fact, many district court judges prefer to conduct voir dire themselves without the inclusion of the parties' counsel due to a commonly held belief that jurors are more forthcoming with judges than counsel and in the interest of more closely controlling the scope of voir dire.[28]

Even before the lawyers ask a single question, the California Code of Civil Procedure states that trial judges "should allow a brief opening statement by counsel for each party. . . ."[29] During this opening statement, counsel can provide a short introduction to the prospective jurors about the basic facts in the underlying matter.

California statute mandates that trial judges then "permit liberal and probing examination" by the parties of prospective jurors.[30] The parties are allowed wide scope to ask about any subjects or information calculated to discover bias or prejudice with regard to the facts at issue in the specific case that the parties are trying.[31] Counsel "should be allowed to ask questions reasonably designed to assist in the intelligent exercise of peremptory challenges whether or not such questions are also likely to uncover grounds sufficient to sustain a challenge for cause."[32] This means that the questioning of jurors need not solely be restricted to questions designed to elicit a response evidencing bias or prejudice. Counsel can generally ask questions that are peripherally related to the question of bias. The court can even permit the parties to ask leading as well as hypothetical questions.[33] This wide latitude in subject matter on which counsel can question prospective jurors even includes repetitive and duplicative questions covering topics upon which the trial court has already questioned the jurors.[34]

Also in contrast to the complete discretion that federal court judges have to control voir dire, judges in California courts are restricted from utilizing any unreasonable or arbitrary time limits for questioning and from utilizing a blanket policy of a time limit for voir dire.[35] Further, California trial court judges may even allow lawyers to conduct voir dire outside of the court's presence when the parties stipulate it. [36] There is an exception to these rules for expedited civil trials, where all of voir dire can only last one hour and each side is given only 15 minutes to complete all of their questioning.[37]

Aside from oral questioning, parties are allowed to submit written questionnaires to the prospective jurors. Trial court judges are allowed to restrict the use of written questionnaires but they are restricted from doing so on an arbitrary or unreasonable basis.[38]

Do not be misled by the preceding paragraphs into thinking that California court's liberal voir dire policy is without restriction. California law still delineates what questions are improper for voir dire. Such questions consist of any that improperly attempt to "indoctrinate the jury, or question the prospective jurors concerning the pleadings or the applicable law."[39] This being said, it is proper to ask prospective jurors whether they agree that it is important for them to apply the law as the court instructs them to.[40] Further, "a reasonable question about the potential juror's willingness to apply a particular doctrine of law should be permitted when from the nature of the case, the judge is satisfied that the doctrine is likely to be relevant at trial."[41]

An example of a specific type of question that is generally improper is a question about a potential juror's religious belief.[42] However, there are circumstantial exceptions. A lawyer can question a person about their religious belief when "the state of mind of a prospective juror, resulting from religious belief, or any other cause, might disqualify such person from acting as a juror in a particular case, regardless of the question of general competency to act as a juror."[43] It is also improper for parties to discuss information for which the parties will not be allowed to provide evidence, such as information barred by the collateral source rule or information concerning settlement efforts.[44]

This rule does not exclude questions whose function is only improper, in part. A question that legitimately seeks to gain information that could lead to a peremptory challenge is still fair game even if the practical result of the question is that it will improperly educate the prospective jurors.[45]

If counsel does ask an improper question, then the trial judge has the right to require that lawyer to stop voir dire and to instead submit all voir dire questions to the court so that the court can review the questions before the lawyer asks them to the prospective jurors.[46] Additionally, opposing counsel may object to the question. If a trial judge does not intervene to stop the improper questioning and the opposing counsel fails to object, then the opposing counsel's failure constitutes a waiver of the improper voir dire.[47]

Voir dire officially finishes when the jury is sworn in regardless of whether each side has used all of their peremptory challenges.[48] Keep in mind that each county has their own local rules that might affect voir dire. For example, Los Angeles Superior Court Local Rule ("Local Rule") 3.48(a) governs pre voir dire conferences between the parties and the court and allows the court and the parties to allow or limit usually improper voir dire questions. Local Rule 3.48(b) also allows for such a pretrial conference to determine the text of a brief statement that the judge can read to the panel of prospective jurors prior to voir dire. At these pretrial conferences, the parties can agree to a panel of less than 12 jurors and can determine the number of alternate jurors.[49] Further, the Los Angeles Superior Court Local Rules mandate that where a party wishes for a trial judge to ask the prospective jurors specific questions, the party must prepare and submit the proposed questions in writing to the court and the opposing party.[50] These are just examples of the local rules in Los Angeles Superior Court but the local rules affecting voir dire will be different depending in which California court a case is being tried.

Voir dire in California's civil courts is fairly liberal, but there is a limit on acceptable activity. If practitioners keep these boundaries in mind and focus on the county specific local rules for the county in which they are conducting their trial, then they can confidently be free to focus on the art and strategy of voir dire, a subject covered by hundreds, if not more, of other articles.

In addition to learning about the potential jurors, voir dire is your first opportunity to develop themes with the jury. Ask potential jurors about their own insurance policies. Do they have any insurance policies? What kind of insurance do they have? Why did they buy insurance? What would they want to happen if they submitted a claim? This focuses the jurors on the nature of insurance and the vulnerability that all claimants face. What good or bad experiences have the potential jurors had with insurance companies? Many are eager to explain their bad experiences with insurers. You must know their feelings about insurers to determine whether you want them on your jury.

Damages is another crucial subject to explore with potential jurors. Many people do not believe in awarding noneconomic damages, let alone punitive damages. You can present a great liability case that results in a small verdict because jurors do not believe in awarding noneconomic or punitive damages. Where jurors believe that punitive damage awards are too high, agree with them and then discuss the purpose of punitive damages—to punish and deter. Find out if the jurors believe in punitive damages when the evidence supports a finding of malice, oppression or fraud. Emphasize that your case is different than the seemingly silly cases that jurors have read about in newspapers.

Tort reform is another essential topic to address. Despite the facts, tort reform marketing campaigns have led many people to believe that lawsuits are out of control. Many jurors now distrust plaintiffs and assume that they are unfairly seeking a big payday. Find out whether the jurors, or anyone they know, have been involved in litigation. A juror who has been a defendant in a lawsuit may have a different perspective than a juror who has been a plaintiff.

It can be very helpful to ask potential jurors what newspapers and magazines they read on a regular basis. A person who reads *The Wall Street Journal* probably will have a different philosophical outlook than someone who reads *The National Enquirer.* The same concept applies to radio and television programs. A Rush Limbaugh fan will generally have a different perspective than a National Public Radio listener.

Juror questionnaires can be helpful in bad faith cases to obtain substantial information about jurors where there is limited time to conduct voir dire. But juror questionnaires frequently benefit the insurers because their counsel can obtain information that they would not feel comfortable asking the potential jurors directly.

Chapter 19: Opening Statement

This chapter will briefly discuss what an opening statement is, the general boundaries of what is proper and improper to include in the opening statement, and the potential consequences for lawyers who push beyond these boundaries. Black's Legal Dictionary points out that opening statements are supposed to be "an advocate's statement giving the fact finder a preview of the case and of the evidence to be presented."[51] While this is the purpose of opening statements, in reality they are used by lawyers as a chance to begin arguing their case directly to the jury. For this reason, people commonly refer to an opening statement as "opening argument."[52] As the California Supreme Court has stated: "An opening statement is precisely what the term implies . . . . Its office is to prepare the minds of the jury to follow the evidence and to more readily discern its materiality, force and effect. The statement is not evidence, and no jury would accept it as facts proved. If [counsel] overstates his case or fails to sustain his opening statement by evidence, or, if, by the court's ruling, the evidence offered to support it is ruled inadmissible, the misfortune or error of judgment is likely to react to his disadvantage." [53]

Ordinarily, opening statements begin immediately after the

court has sworn in the jury.[54] However, trial judges can allow counsel to make an opening statement to a jury panel prior to voir dire, in addition to the opening statements which parties are entitled to make.[55] The plaintiffs are the first party that may give their opening statement and present the issues of their case.[56] They are then followed by the defendants who may state their defense. However, the defendants also have their choice of waiting and presenting their opening statement after the plaintiffs have produced their evidence.[57] The judge can change this prescribed order if the court has "special reason to do so."[58] Further, if there are several defendants and each defendant has a different attorney and different defense, then it is the trial judge's choice as to which one gets to present an opening statement first.[59] This scheme is the same regardless of whether it is a jury or bench trial.[60]

There is no prescribed time limit for how long or short an opening statement should or must be. Trial judges have discretion concerning how much time each party has for their opening statement and such a decision will not be reversed absent a total abuse of discretion.[61] Even in expedited civil trials, the trial judge may allow additional time for the opening statement upon a finding of good cause.[62]

As explained above, an opening statement is not evidence. Therefore, statements that counsel makes in opening arguments will not open the door for the opposing counsel to produce otherwise inadmissible evidence on the topics that are raised in the opening arguments.[63] This is in contrast to many federal courts, including the courts within the Ninth Circuit, which do find that statements made in opening argument can open the door on otherwise not relevant or admissible evidence.[64] It is also not the lawyers' job to instruct the jury as to what the law is but if the court deems that it would be useful for a party to read legal authority to the jury as part of the opening statement, then that judge would have the discretion to allow it.[65]

Counsel cannot discuss in their opening arguments any matters that the trial court has explicitly ruled inadmissible in a prior order. Lawyers are also not allowed to discuss any facts or matters unless they have a reasonable basis for believing that they will tender evidence supporting the facts and that the court will admit the evidence.[66] This means that the lawyers cannot rely upon rank speculation or even worse—known false facts—to mislead the jury during their opening statement. This also means that lawyers cannot mention facts or evidence in their opening argument that are irrelevant or which the lawyers know is not admissible for any other reason.[67]

If an attorney does include such improper argument in their opening statement, then the opposing counsel has multiple ways to seek relief. One such avenue is to immediately object and seek an admonishment by the trial judge to the jury to disregard the improper conduct. Opposing counsel can also seek sanctions for improper opening arguments. [68] Where the opening argument is severely prejudicial, the opposing party can even seek a reversal or new trial.[69]

Rules govern not only what lawyers say during opening argument, but also what they do. For example, in the Los Angeles Superior Court, it is improper for counsel to display to the jury or reference a chart, graph, map, picture, model, video or other graphic device or presentation except in three situations. First, the lawyer can show or reference such items if they are pieces of evidence that the trial judge has received into evidence. Second, the lawyer can present such items by stipulation of the parties. Finally, the arguing attorney can show such items to the jury or reference such items if the court grants them leave to do so.[70] Further, a lawyer can only use a chalkboard or paper for illustrative purposes during their opening statements if they have the prior approval of the trial court judge.[71]

If an opening statement is not improper but merely deficient for failing to describe evidence that constitutes a valid cause of action, then the opposing counsel can move for nonsuit immediately after the argument.[72] Similarly, if a defendant fails to state evidence supporting a defense in their opening statement, then plaintiff can move for a directed verdict immediately after the defendant's opening statement.[73] Trial judges cannot grant such nonsuit or directed verdict motions unless it is clear counsel has stated all of the facts that the party expects to prove during trial and they are still legally insufficient.[74] Further, in these cases where an opposing party files a motion for nonsuit or directed verdict, the party whose opening statement is challenged can request leave to "reopen" the opening arguments to remedy any deficiencies.[75]

Opening statement is the time to establish themes and tell the story. Many attorneys start their opening statements by stating their theme, telling the jury why the case is about their theme, then telling the jury what happened, why it happened and who to believe. As in all storytelling, the opening statement must answer the questions who, what, why, when, where and how. Set the scene and introduce the characters using descriptive and colorful language.

An effective approach is to follow the theme of promises and broken promises focusing on the insurance company's conduct. Show the jury the insurance company's marketing materials such as television commercials and print advertising, and review the company's representations in the insurance policy.

Next, show the jury your client in the best possible light. Tell the jury the policyholder's life story. Emphasize the policyholder's likeable qualities. For example, discuss testimony that will demonstrate that the policyholder is caring, a hard worker, and has good values.

After the jury learns about your client, educate the jury about the relevant insurance industry standards that the insurance company is required to follow in handling claims. Although there are many industry standards, present only the important standards that the defendant has violated. Compile the industry standards from published decisions, statutes, regulations, jury instructions, the insurance contract, the insurer's policies and procedures, industry guidelines, insurance experts, the insurer's written discovery responses, and the insurer's deposition testimony. During discovery, obtain testimony from the insurer's adjusters and the insurer's experts confirming that the insurer is required to follow the relevant industry standards so that you can tell the jury that everyone agrees that the insurer is required to follow these standards (you will later elicit testimony from the defense witnesses confirming this).

Next, review the company's unreasonable handling of the claim. A simple timeline is an effective way to provide the jury with a reference point through which to view the entire claims handling process. The timeline should emphasize the key liability facts that violate the industry standards at issue. Depending upon the specific facts and issues in your case, you may focus on the company's failure to thoroughly investigate the claim, failure to fully inquire into all bases that might support the insured's claim, failure to objectively evaluate the claim, failure to promptly investigate the claim, failure to pay benefits when due, or any other unreasonable conduct.

To maximize the size of the potential punitive damage verdict, focus on facts that will justify a larger punitive damage award. Remember, the degree of reprehensibility of an insurer's conduct is one of the most crucial factors that appellate courts review in evaluating a punitive damages award against an insurer. [76] To consider reprehensibility, a court must consider (1) whether the conduct involved repeated actions or was an isolated incident, (2) whether the harm was the result of intentional malice, trickery, or deceit or simply an accident, (3) whether the harm caused was physical or economic, (4) whether the conduct evidenced an indifference to, or reckless disregard of, the health and safety of others, and (5) whether the target of the conduct had financial vulnerability. As a result, highlight the facts that emphasize these factors.

As in any opening statement, be honest with the jury and do not say anything that you will not prove. For the facts in dispute, explain your client's position, the insurance company's position, and why the client's position is better. Address all of the major weaknesses in your case to diffuse the impact of the defendant's focus on these weaknesses.

To keep the jurors' interest, use a limited number of key exhibits in your opening statement. Computer programs including Sanction, PowerPoint, and Trial Director provide an excellent way to integrate key documents, blowups, and deposition testimony into your opening statement.

Chapter 20: Direct and Cross Examination

Generally, the presentation of witnesses should reflect the trial theme and roughly mirror the story that you told in opening statement. But strategic considerations will dictate the order of witnesses in each case. Streamline your case so that it is simple and hard hitting from start to finish. Consequently, keep the case moving efficiently by only calling witnesses who are absolutely necessary to the case.

If the plaintiff makes a great witness, consider calling the plaintiff first. After humanizing the plaintiff, review the promises the plaintiff relied upon before he bought insurance. Then review the loss and the insurer's unreasonable handling of the claim. Spend a substantial amount of time addressing all of the damages that the plaintiff suffered in detail. The plaintiff is the victim.

Sometimes it may be appropriate to call the insurance company adjusters early in your case. Start by having the adjusters confirm that they are required to comply with the industry standards that you listed in opening statement. Then lead them to confirm key facts that help the case. After using the adjusters to acknowledge helpful facts, elicit testimony that establishes the insurer's violations of the industry standards. The same logic applies to the insurer's experts.

The plaintiff's insurance expert can be an effective witness to close the plaintiff's case. They generally begin by explaining the industry standards supporting the implied covenant of good faith and fair dealing. The expert can then explain the unequal bargaining positions of insurance companies and policyholders and the unique nature of the relationship. Following the general discussion, the expert lists all of the insurance company's unreasonable conduct in handling the claim.

Chapter 21: Closing Argument

Closing argument is the opportunity to retell your story through the evidence. As the jury has already heard the evidence, review the key evidence that supports a bad faith verdict and punitive damages.

Start with your list of industry standards that the insurance company violated. For each standard, review the evidence that proves that the insurer violated that standard. The evidence should include the key documents and trial testimony. Instead of telling the jury your recollections of the evidence, show the jury the specific documents and trial testimony that support the violations. Let the evidence speak for itself. PowerPoint, Sanction and Trial Director provide great formats through which to communicate the industry standards and evidence.

After reviewing the violations of industry standards, walk the jurors through the key jury instructions. Review the relevant bad faith jury instructions and then show the jury a detailed summary of the insurer's unreasonable conduct that supports a bad faith verdict. Review the punitive damage jury instructions and provide the jury with a list of the insurer's conduct that was malicious, oppressive or fraudulent.

At the end of the closing argument, empower the jury by reminding them that they are the voice of the community and they have the power to stop similar conduct from occurring in the future.

Finally, the key to trying a bad faith case, like trying any other type of case, is preparation. Before you step into the courtroom, you must know the relevant facts and law better than anyone else. Thorough preparation will give you the essential background and confidence to maximize your performance during each stage of trial. It also is necessary to build credibility, the most important characteristic of a trial lawyer.

SECTION IV: DAMAGES

Damages in insurance bad faith cases are generally straight forward. There are three levels to the analysis – breach of contract, breach of the implied covenant of good faith and fair dealing (bad faith), and punitive damages.

Chapter 22: Damages Arising Out of the Insurance Contract

Where a plaintiff establishes a breach of contract, generally the damages will be the policy benefits plus interest from the date that the benefits were due.[77] Thus, in first party cases the damage will be the contract benefits plus interest. In third party cases, the damage will be the amount expended or liability incurred by the policyholder up to the policy limit, plus foreseeable consequential damages. Where an insurer wrongfully refuses to provide a defense to its insured, the damage will include the cost that the insured incurred to defend the action. In cases involving insurance that directly affects the comfort, happiness or personal welfare of the insured, or that involve a subject matter that affects the self-esteem or feelings of that party, emotional distress damages may be recoverable as foreseeable damages.[78]

To recover for bad faith damages, the plaintiff must prove that the insurance company breached the insurance contract by withholding, delaying or denying benefits in bad faith.[79] Where a plaintiff proves bad faith, the measure of damages will be tort damages. The plaintiff will be entitled to recover for all damage proximately caused by the insurer's bad faith.[80]

These damages are recoverable regardless of whether or not the damage could have been anticipated, in contrast to consequential damages in breach of contract, which must have been within the contemplation of the parties when the contract was entered into. Bad faith damages typically include economic damage, emotional distress, attorneys' fees and prejudgment interest.

Economic damage will include all economic losses that the plaintiff suffered as a result of the insurer's bad faith. Emotional distress damages will include the emotional distress that the plaintiff suffered as a consequence of the insurer's bad faith conduct. But in order to recover for emotional distress damages, plaintiff must have suffered some threshold economic loss, for example medical treatment resulting from the emotional distress, attorneys' fees or some costs of litigation.[81] When claiming emotional distress, it is wise to have family members, friends and treating providers who witnessed the distress testify about the emotional distress.

Plaintiff can also recover the cost of the attorneys' fees incurred in establishing that plaintiff is entitled to contract benefits. But plaintiff cannot recover for attorneys' fees incurred in establishing the insurer's bad faith or in establishing that the plaintiff is entitled to punitive damages.[82] Where plaintiff's counsel is working for a contingency fee, plaintiff has the burden of proving their entitlement to attorneys' fees and must establish the amount of the attorneys' fees incurred in an effort to obtain policy benefits.[83] Normally this is an issue for the jury, but counsel often stipulate to have the judge adjudicate this issue after a finding of bad faith.

Chapter 23: Punitive Damages Arising out of Bad Faith

Once a plaintiff has established that an insurer has denied benefits in bad faith, the door to potential recovery of punitive damages is opened. Under California law, before a plaintiff can recover punitive damages, he must prove, by clear and convincing evidence, fraud, malice or oppression by the defendant as laid out in Civ. Code section 3294(c). Under this clear and convincing evidence standard, there must be a strong probability that the facts giving rise to the fraud, malice or oppression occurred.[84]

In order to recover punitive damages, you must prove that the bad faith conduct was authorized or ratified by the insurance company. Specifically, plaintiff must prove that an officer, director or managing agent "had the requisite advance knowledge and conscious disregard," "authorized or ratified the employee's acts," or acted with oppression, fraud or malice toward the injured party.[85]

The award of punitive damages lies solely in the province of the jury, and recent case law reaffirms that the court cannot influence whether or not a jury awards punitive damages.[86]

The United States Supreme Court's jurisprudence over the past decade has had an impact on getting and, more importantly, keeping punitive damage awards. But the power that punitive damages have to change corporate conduct has not totally disappeared. The Supreme Court's more recent cases have clarified and changed the focus on some issues—and if you pursue those issues, you will lay the groundwork for getting and keeping substantial punitive damages.[87]

Although the principles discussed below are all derived from the Supreme Court's decisions, most have not yet been tested in practice. But that certainly does not mean that you should not try them or that they will not succeed. So long as we continue to push the envelope, and use the tools we have, we can do what needs to be done to protect people from overreaching by corporations that do not honor their responsibilities to their customers.

Reprehensibility Is the Key

Although the U.S. Supreme Court has used various means of disposing of punitive damages awards, every decision has been predicated on the issue of "fair notice." That means that, constitutionally, the defendant is entitled to have fair notice of what conduct will potentially subject it to punitive damages and the extent of the damages that can rationally be expected to be imposed on the basis of that conduct. Of the three "guideposts" that the court frequently discusses, it consistently emphasizes that the "reprehensibility" guidepost is the most important. The key for plaintiffs' attorneys is to know what that means, in the context of fair notice, and to use it at every turn.

The reprehensibility factors that have evolved from the case law include:

- Economic v. physical harm (Note: the Utah Supreme Court concluded that economic harm that causes emotional distress is more reprehensible than mere economic harm.);
- Indifference or reckless disregard of health or safety;
- Financial vulnerability of the plaintiff;
- Pattern and practice;
- Recidivism;
- Malice, trickery, and deceit versus "mere" accident;
- The scale of profitability;
- Profit motivation;
- Similar, out-of-state conduct;
- Impact on the state; and
- Impact on others

Some of these issues are the usual run-of-the-mill topics we deal with in trying punitive damages cases, i.e., trickery, deceit and reckless disregard (or, in California, conscious disregard). But some of these issues are new and different and open up new vistas in discovery and the evidence to use at trial.

While highly reprehensible conduct may lead to larger punitive damages awards, the reverse is also true. Where the degree of reprehensibility of the defendant's conduct is relatively low, the permissible award ratio of compensatory to punitive damages will be lower. For example, if a compensatory damages award includes substantial compensation for physical and emotional distress (which tends to suggest that the jury intended to punish the defendant), but the defendant's reprehensibility is relatively low, one court concluded that the maximum constitutionally permissible punitive damages award ratio of compensatory to punitive damages may be set at 1:1. [88]

Pattern and Practice

As already explained above in detail, California insurance law cases can utilize a well-developed body of law that permits discovery of, and submission of evidence on, pattern and practice of improper insurance claims handling.[89] The case law makes clear that pattern and practice is relevant to the reprehensibility analysis.

Recidivism

The U.S. Supreme Court has repeatedly stated that a recidivist defendant deserves to be punished more harshly. That means you should get discovery on:

• Other compensatory or punitive damages awards against the defendant regarding the same conduct with respect to the claim you have.

• Other compensatory or punitive damage awards against the defendant even with respect to other policies or other type of claims. This may seem anti-intuitive in light of the court's decision in *State Farm* - but remember, we are talking about fair notice. Irrespective of the specific type of claim involved, if the defendant was "dinged" before for substantially similar conduct, even in a different context, it had fair notice of the type of conduct that would get it in trouble and the level of punishment that could be involved. Plus, if there have been other actions against the defendant and it did not change its ways before injuring your insured, it is a recidivist and needs to be punished more severely.

• Look for civil penalties or government or regulatory action. If an insurer has been fined anywhere for conduct similar to that at issue in your case, and hasn't changed its conduct—it is a recidivist. And again, the evidence goes to fair notice. Look for such fines or regulatory action with other state insurance departments and the FTC (regarding advertising issues).

Scale of Profitability

In *Johnson v. Ford Motor Co.* (2005) 35 Cal.4th 1191, the California Supreme Court held that evidence gained from the defendant's wrongful conduct cannot be recovered as mere disgorgement. But, the court held, the amount of money made by the defendant as the result of engaging in the unfair conduct is admissible as part of the reprehensibility analysis.

Profit Motivation

A recent case under federal common law looked to profit motivation as a factor in determining the reprehensibility of a defendant's conduct. In *Exon Shipping Co. v. Baker*, 554 U.S. 471, 494 (2008), the court held "[a]ction taken or omitted in order to augment profit represents an enhanced degree of culpability."

State's Interest

This is a particularly new and novel approach, and is only worth pursuing in really significant cases, but if it applies, it might turn out to be a very powerful weapon.

The analysis here starts with language from *State Farm* which was expanded upon in the Utah Supreme Court's decision after remand from the U.S. Supreme Court. Essentially, the analysis is based on the fact that each individual state has an interest in imposing punitive damages in order to protect its own interest and the interests of its citizens. The impact the defendant's conduct has on the state and its citizens as a whole is an assessment that the jury can properly consider in determining reprehensibility.

There is a three-step process for the analysis:

(a) Define the scope of the legitimate state interests the punitive damages award is intended to further;

(b) Discover the potential impact of the defendants' conduct on that interest; and

(c) Calculate the financial impact on the state.

As an example, the scope of a state's interest in the context of an insurance claim is to assure the financial security and independence of its citizens and/or to provide protection to assets. A state is always interested in assuring that competition is protected because if the marketplace is not trustworthy, the economic impact will be disastrous. Propound discovery on the impact the defendant's conduct is likely to have in the marketplace. Find out how many of the same or similar types of policies have been sold by defendant in the state and the size of its market share. Find out how many claims are associated with that policy type, by both the defendant and, to the extent you can, competitors. Also dig out information about the frequency of claims denied for the same or similar reasons on the same or similar kinds of policies. Once you have that kind of economic information, get a forensic economist to do a calculation of the harm to competitors and the harm to the economy that has, or would, result if the defendant were allowed to continue the conduct.

There is one important thing to note here. As discussed in the next section on harm to others, you must be sure to tell the jury, through argument and instructions, that it may not award an amount of punitive damages that will reimburse the state for these losses. They can only consider the evidence in determining the reprehensibility of the defendant's conduct. But since the instructions should—consistent with the Supreme Court's jurisprudence—tell the jury that the reprehensibility factor is the most important one, it may well have a profound effect on the jury's perspective.

Harm to Others

Another instructive case is *Philip Morris v. Williams*, 127 S.Ct. 1057 (2007). The most important thing that came out of the *Williams* case was the line it drew. It held that a jury's award of punitive damages could not include an amount for harm to others, but that the evidence of harm to others could be included in the jury's assessment of the reprehensibility of the defendant's conduct (which is, again, the most important factor in determining whether the punitive damages are constitutionally acceptable).

This is conceptually hard to understand. In fact, Justice Stevens in his concurring and dissenting opinion said that "the nuance escapes me." But be that as it may, what it means is that you can get the evidence before the jury, so long as you are careful to instruct the jury that it may only consider the evidence for purposes of reprehensibility and may not award an amount that actually represents the harm to others.

Chapter 24: Crafting Punitive Damage Jury Instructions

Because of these nuances, the jury instructions in a punitive damages case take on much more importance. There is no point trying to dance around the issues. Take them head on and tell the jury they cannot award any amount of punitive damages to reimburse the state or others who have been harmed. But also tell them that they can take these issues into consideration in deciding the reprehensibility of the conduct and that reprehensibility is the most important factor.

If you think you have a good shot at getting to the punitive damages, you should also be sure to instruct the jury that noneconomic damages should not include any punitive aspect, in order to avoid the problems on that issue from the State Farm decision.

SECTION V: BAD FAITH CASES AGAINST HMOS

As explained earlier, an HMO is a type of health care service plan that is licensed and regulated by the California Department of Managed Health Care.[90] HMOs arrange for the provision of medical services in exchange for periodic premium payments. They issue contracts to their insureds, referred to as subscribers or members, called an Evidence of Coverage ("EOC"). The EOCs promise to provide covered medical services. HMOs are different than traditional health insurers in that they arrange for the provision of medical services while traditional health insurers simply pay for medical services. Traditional health insurers are licensed and regulated by the Department of Insurance under the Insurance Code. But HMOs are specifically exempted from the jurisdiction of the Department of Insurance and the Insurance Code.[91] Because of the differences between traditional insurance companies and HMOs, the strategies and techniques for building a case against an HMO also differs from building a case against a traditional insurer.

Chapter 25: The HMOs' Financial Incentive to Withhold Care

In California, most HMOs operate through a delegated model of delivering health care services. Under this model, the HMOs do not directly employ healthcare providers to treat their subscribers. Instead, the HMOs enter contracts with groups of physicians called Participating Medical Groups or Independent Practice Associations ("IPAs") to provide medical services to subscribers. The IPAs then enter into separate contracts with physicians, including primary care physicians and specialists, to treat subscribers.

These contracts provide financial incentives to delay and deny care. The HMOs' contracts with IPAs, commonly called IPA Services Agreements, essentially transform the IPAs into small insurance companies with financial incentives to deny care. In exchange for payments from the HMOs, the IPAs normally agree to determine what medical care a subscriber requires and whether that care is covered under the HMO's EOC. Most importantly, the IPAs agree to provide or pay for most of the medical care that a subscriber needs.

The IPA Services Agreements often provide the IPAs with two forms of financial incentives to deny care: capitation payments and risk-sharing pools. Capitation payments are fixed monthly payments based solely upon the number of subscribers that the HMO assigns to an IPA. For example, an HMO may pay an IPA $200 per month for each subscriber assigned to that IPA. The IPA receives the capitation payment regardless of whether the subscriber is healthy or sick. If the subscriber is healthy, and requires no medical care, the IPA receives $200 for the subscriber without having to pay for any medical care. If the subscriber is extremely sick, and requires substantial care, the IPA must pay for the expensive care although it still only receives $200 per month for the subscriber. Capitation is legal and authorized by statute.[92]

HMOs also establish risk-sharing pools to limit the utilization of certain medical services. Risk sharing involves transferring the cost of medical services from the HMOs to the IPAs and healthcare providers. For example, some HMOs withhold a percentage of an IPA's capitation payments at the beginning of each year and place the money into a risk-sharing pool that is earmarked for certain services, such as in-patient hospital stays. The HMO then develops a budget for the anticipated cost of the hospital stays for the members assigned to the IPA. At the end of the year, if the actual cost of the hospital stays for the members exceeds the budget, the IPA will be financially responsible for some of the additional cost. If the actual cost is less than the budget, the IPA receives a percentage of the money left in the risk-sharing pool. Because the HMOs have tremendous bargaining power over the IPAs, many IPAs are in financial trouble and several have filed bankruptcy.

The delegated model also provides treating physicians with financial incentives to deny care. Many IPAs enter capitation contracts with primary care physicians and specialists. As a result, physicians have financial incentives to maintain large patient populations under their care. To handle the large patient populations, many primary care physicians employ nurse practitioners to treat subscribers. The capitation contracts often require physicians to directly or indirectly pay for part of the cost of certain expensive services such as diagnostic procedures. The physicians, therefore, have a financial incentive to limit the number of diagnostic procedures that they order for subscribers. Moreover, physicians often have ownership interests in IPAs and have incentives to make the IPAs profitable. Many capitated primary care physicians and specialists receive bonuses based on an IPA's profitability.

The most important defendant is the HMO. The potential causes of action to assert against an HMO include breach of contract, bad faith, unfair business practices, fraud, negligent misrepresentation, wrongful death and intentional and negligent infliction of emotional distress.

The IPA is usually also a proper defendant. The strongest potential cause of action to allege against the IPA is tortious interference with the EOC based upon a theory that the IPA interfered with the EOC by improperly denying or delaying covered medical care for its own financial gain.[93] Additionally, the IPA can be liable for breach of fiduciary duty for failing to disclose financial incentives that may affect coverage decisions.[94]

Chapter 26: Discovery Specific to HMO Cases

To prove that an HMO handled the requests for care unreasonably and maliciously, oppressively or fraudulently, establish that the HMO violated its duties to the member based on the HMO's promises in the EOC, published bad faith decisions, statutes, regulations, and industry standards.

The National Committee for Quality Assurance ("NCQA") is an accrediting body that accredits managed care organizations. It annually publishes a set of industry standards for HMOs titled Standards for the Accreditation of Managed Care Organizations ("NCQA standards"). HMOs seek accreditation from the NCQA to help sell their products. NCQA accreditation, according to one HMO's advertising materials, is like the Good Housekeeping Seal of Approval. In order to obtain NCQA accreditation, an HMO must promise to comply with the NCQA's standards. The NCQA standards provide fertile ground for establishing that the HMO violated its duties to the member.

To develop a case in discovery, pay particular attention to the following areas:

HMOs have a duty to thoroughly investigate requests for

care and fully inquire into all possible bases that might support the request for care.[95] Explore the ways that the HMO could have fully investigated the request, and then contrast that with the investigation that the HMO or IPA actually conducted. The utilization review process is the process through which HMOs and IPAs evaluate requests for care. Obtain all of the defendants' documents regarding utilization review relating to the member. Also obtain their policies and procedures relating to utilization review. Then depose the decision-makers to find out exactly what investigation they conducted. Find out why they decided to delay or deny the request for care and what documents they read, reviewed or relied upon before making the decision. Often, the individual or individuals who made the decision to delay or deny the care never reviewed any of the member's medical records, spoke with the member or talked with the member's treating physicians.

HMOs have a duty to promptly respond to requests for care. This is a crucial issue for several reasons. First, subscribers often require prompt treatment. For example, cancer patients may have a short window of opportunity within which to receive appropriate care before their cancer metastasizes and causes further damage. But HMOs operating through a delegated model have created a system that encourages delays. Physicians and subscribers must overcome layers of bureaucracy to obtain authorization for services. Normally all requests for treatment must be submitted by a subscriber's primary care physician. In many states, it is common for HMO patients to have to wait weeks for an appointment with their primary care physician. Once a subscriber visits their primary care physician, the physician is required to submit a request for authorization to an IPA for the member to receive additional services, such as diagnostic tests or referrals to specialists. It can take days to weeks for an IPA to decide whether to authorize the requested service, and IPAs often ask primary care physicians to submit additional information before they will make a decision. If the IPA approves the request, there is often a delay before the service can be scheduled. If the IPA denies the request, the subscriber can appeal to the HMO. Excluding emergencies, it normally takes HMOs one month to decide whether to uphold or reverse the denial.

In contrast to these delays, NCQA standards include turnaround times for responding to requests for care. NCQA Standard UM 4 provides that HMOs must make decisions regarding request for non-urgent care within two working days of obtaining the necessary information and decisions regarding urgent care within one working day of obtaining the necessary information. Health & Safety Code section 1367.01 requires HMOs to make utilization review decisions when a member faces an imminent and serious threat to his health within 72 hours after the HMO's receipt of the relevant information, and make decisions regarding other requests for care within 5 business days.

HMOs have a duty to ensure that qualified health professionals make utilization review decisions. NCQA Standard UM 3 provides that "qualified health professionals assess the clinical information used to support [utilization review] decisions." Additionally, an HMO must have procedures for "using board-certified physicians from appropriate specialty areas to assist in making determinations of medical necessity." Health & Safety Code § 1367.01(e) provides that only a licensed physician or health care provider "who is competent to evaluate the specific clinical issues involved in the health care services requested" may deny a request for care based on medical necessity. HMOs must communicate decisions to delay, deny or modify requests for care in writing and provide a clear and concise explanation of the reasons for the HMO's decision, a description of the criteria or guidelines used, and clinical reasons for decisions regarding medical necessity.[96]

HMOs have a duty to provide continuity of care and coordination of care.[97] An HMO must ensure that the member receives continuous care from the same physicians and is not shuffled from doctor to doctor during the member's treatment. An HMO must also make sure that a physician is coordinating the member's care. Members with a complicated disease process, such as cancer, often require several different specialists. An HMO must have a physician assigned to coordinate the member's care and ensure that the treating physicians are communicating with each other regarding the patient.

HMOs have a duty to provide members with referrals to specialists that are consistent with good professional practice.[98] Referring subscribers to specialists costs HMOs and IPAs money. As a result, primary care physicians are often reluctant to refer members to specialists when it is medically appropriate. Additionally, HMOs require members to treat with their contracted physicians. HMOs are extremely hesitant to refer members to non-contracted physicians because the HMOs then can lose control over the costs of the member's care.

Historically, HMOs' utilization review obligations were non-delegable. Where HMOs delegate the utilization-review functions to IPAs, IPAs often make the initial decisions to delay or deny the requests for care without any involvement of the HMO. Unfortunately, in these situations, the current state of the law in California is that the IPAs are independent contractors and, therefore, the HMO is not liable for the IPA's conduct.

However, the case of *Kotler v. PacifiCare of California*, 126 Cal.App.4th 950 (2005) is instructive. *Kotler* involved a PacifiCare member who was enrolled in a PacifiCare HMO that delegated utilization review decisions to a medical group.

Under the PacifiCare HMO, the plaintiff had a primary care physician who was responsible for directing and coordinating his medical care. The plaintiff sued PacifiCare for breach of contract and bad faith for making him wait an unreasonable length of time to obtain an appointment to see a specialist – even though the plaintiff only dealt with his medical group and had no contact with PacifiCare regarding the appointment.

The court held that PacifiCare could be liable for bad faith based on the failure of its delegated medical group to provide a timely appointment with a specialist. The case recognized that PacifiCare had an implied-in-law obligation to provide its members with timely treatment. The Court reached this result even though PacifiCare had not made the appointment at issue and the plaintiff did not seek PacifiCare's assistance in getting a quicker appointment. The court noted that PacifiCare's plan stated that it was the primary care physician who would coordinate plaintiff's care and make referrals to specialists, and the plaintiff had sought the primary care physician's assistance.

Chapter 27: HMOs Are Subject to Bad Faith Liability

Historically, HMOs have argued that they are not subject to tort liability for their unreasonable denial of medical care because they are not insurance companies. But case law has closed the door on this defense. In *Rush Prudential HMO, Inc. v. Moran*, 536 U.S 355, 122 S.Ct. 2151, 153 L.Ed.2d 375 (2002), the Supreme Court confirmed that an HMO "provides health care ... as an insurer." The Court noted that an HMO cannot "checkmate common sense by trying to submerge HMOs' insurance features beneath an exclusive characterization of HMOs as providers of health care." Also see *Smith v. PacifiCare*, 93 Cal.App.4th 139; 157-158; 113 Cal.Rptr.2d 140, 153 (2001)[HMOs are engaged in providing a service that is a substitute for what previously constituted health insurance, and are in the business of insurance].

The HMO's parent company will contend that it is a separate company and had no involvement with the decision to delay or deny the medical care. To combat this defense, establish that the parent company is in a joint venture with its subsidiary to operate the HMO. Because each joint venturer is the agent for the other members of the venture, all members are liable for the torts committed by any venturer while acting in connection with the venture.[99] If the parent company is a publicly traded company, its SEC 10-K filings should provide admissions regarding its involvement in the subsidiary's business.

SECTION VI: OBAMACARE' S IMPACT ON CONSUMER RIGHTS

The Patient Protection and Affordable Care Act (ACA) — i.e., Obamacare — has created controversy and spurred national debate over the law's insurance mandate. The ACA stretches over 900 pages, contains hundreds of provisions, and provides many new rules governing health insurers. But how will the ACA affect the rights of health insurance policyholders?

Chapter 28: Bad Faith Litigation Prior to the ACA

Consumers faced two common recurring problems before the ACA. First, insurers refused to insure applicants or rescinded policyholders' coverage due to preexisting conditions. Second, insurers improperly delayed and denied coverage for medically necessary treatment.

A preexisting condition is a medical condition that someone has before applying for health insurance. Some conditions, like cancer or HIV, are life-threatening. But health insurers have denied coverage to people with hay fever, asthma, a sports injury, or even being a survivor of domestic violence. Health insurers have used preexisting conditions to deny insureds' treatment by rescinding their coverage for preexisting conditions. This is known as "post claims underwriting." The practice of denying or rescinding coverage based on a preexisting condition has forced millions of the most vulnerable Americans to either go without necessary treatment or face financial ruin.

Health insurers also have a history of wrongfully delaying and denying coverage for autism, eating disorders, cancer, mental health disorders and organ transplants.

Chapter 29: What the ACA Contains

Before delving into the question of how, if at all, the ACA addresses such substantial issues, it is important to understand broadly what the ACA contains. The ACA changes the way the government regulates health insurance and the way people consume health insurance services. The act is divided into 10 titles which generally cover four major changes to the U.S. health insurance system. These changes include: (1) a mandate which requires businesses and individuals to carry a baseline level of health insurance or pay a penalty; (2) a system of federal subsidies to completely or partially pay for the health insurance that is now required for about 34 million Americans who are currently uninsured; (3) new requirements on the health insurance industry; and (4) numerous regulations on the practice of medicine.

Some of these provisions are designed to keep premium costs down while keeping quality high. Specifically, the ACA implemented a higher medical loss ratio rule, which requires insurers to spend 80 to 85 percent of premium dollars on medical care, rather than on administrative costs. If they don't, the insurers must provide a rebate to their customers. In addition, the act restricts companies from putting lifetime limits on a patient's health benefits.

The ACA prohibits health insurers from discriminating against anyone based on their prior medical conditions. Specifically, the act explicitly prohibits discrimination against individuals based on their health status, medical condition (including both physical and mental illnesses), claims experience, receipt of health care, medical history, genetic information, evidence of insurability (including conditions arising out of acts of domestic violence), disability, or any other health status-related factor.

The ACA reforms health plans' internal appeals processes for denied claims. This regulation requires that group health and insurance plans: "(A) have in effect an internal claims appeal process; (B) provide notice to enrollees, in a culturally and linguistically appropriate manner, of available internal and external appeals processes, and the availability of any applicable office of health insurance consumer assistance or ombudsman to assist such enrollees with the appeals processes; and (C) allow an enrollee to review their file, to present evidence and testimony as part of the appeals process, and to receive continued coverage pending the outcome of the appeals process." It also mandates that plans provide an external review process as well. Specifically, it states that group health plans and health insurers shall comply with the applicable state external review process for such plans. This appeal scheme will apply to both state-regulated and ERISA-regulated plans, and thus will end the varied protections that only apply in some states and to some plans.

Chapter 30: The Effects of the ACA Regulations

The ACA enhances the current appeals regulations in California. California has two regulatory systems: one run by the California Department of Insurance, which governs health insurance carriers, and another run by the Department of Managed Health Care (DMHC), which governs health care service plans pursuant to the Knox-Keene Act. Health care service plans are required to maintain internal grievance procedures approved by the DMHC, and to resolve grievances within 30 days, explaining in writing the reasons for any delay or denial of health care services. Unlike the ACA, California statutes do not specifically state that the health plans allow for the presentation of evidence or testimony (although this should be required by the implied covenant of good faith and fair dealing). Under California's regulatory scheme, a consumer can also file complaints directly with the DMHC. The DMHC can determine that the dispute is subject to a separate independent medical review if it involves a determination of whether a treatment is medically necessary. If not, then the DMHC can issue its own findings and determination within 30 calendar days of receipt of the grievance.

This being said, while the ACA expands regulation of the

claim and coverage appeals processes, it does not provide consumers with any new private right to enforce the regulatory provisions of the ACA. Instead, enforcement of the regulations of the ACA is given solely to the states. When health insurers or health plans wrong consumers, then those consumers are still forced to sue in a court of law for redress under theories including breach of contract and bad faith. The act does not affect the way those lawsuits will be brought and does not provide the opportunity for those consumers to seek redress under any new statutory authority or cause of action. The ACA explicitly does not reduce the effects of ERISA preemption on such state law cases or expand consumers' opportunity to sue for punitive damages. The ACA also does not touch upon many roadblocks that consumers face when bringing such bad faith actions. Specifically, the ACA does not address prevalence of mandatory pre-dispute arbitration clauses that often force consumers into unfair arbitration models.

While the act sets out additional protections for consumers through the regulatory framework that it imposes, it does not provide consumers with any new tools to ultimately fix problems that persist when health insurers improperly delay or deny treatment. At the end of the day, the health insurers are still in control of whether they will approve or deny the treatments that our doctors recommend.

SECTION VII: EXAMPLES OF BAD FAITH CASES

What follows are two cases that I brought on behalf of people who were the victims of bad faith. Their stories, I hope, illustrate my perspective and unique approach for addressing bad faith cases.

Chapter 31: Edward Nome's Story

Edward[100] was a poor immigrant who came to this country at the age of twenty. He started selling umbrellas on street corners in New York for a dollar. Fast forward forty years, and Edward lives in Malibu, California and owns shopping centers throughout Southern California. He embodied the American dream. Edward worked hard and paid for health insurance. But when Edward developed hepatitis and end-stage liver disease, his insurer turned its back on him. He needed a liver transplant. His insurer authorized him to receive a liver transplant at a local contracted university ("University"). Edward's University doctor told him that he should go to Texas for a quicker transplant because he may not survive the one-to-two year wait for a transplant at the University. Unfortunately, the doctor failed to note his recommendation in any of the medical records.

Edward chose to live and moved to Texas for the transplant. He asked that his insurer pay for the transplant. After the insurer's own transplant case manager internally recommended that the insurer cover the transplant, a medical director denied the transplant. So Edward paid for the transplant himself and made a great recovery. Edward returned to California and appealed the denial to his insurer several times, and it repeatedly denied the appeal on the ground that the transplant was out-of-network and the out-of-state transplant was not medically necessary.

Edward hired me to sue the insurer. His goal wasn't to get his money back; he wanted to win a judgment against the insurer to keep it from denying a life-saving procedure to another patient. I knew that we had the fundamentals of a great story that I needed to effectively communicate to a jury.

Preparing for Trial

I wanted to find the emotional core of the story. I started our journey doing reenactments with my client. I met with Edward and his family at their home. Together with family members, we reenacted moments during his illness before the transplant. Through the reenactments, I was able to see the vivid image of his body like a starving child – skinny with a huge belly. As he reenacted his attempts to sleep, he showed me how he gasped for breath when lying down. These images became the means through which I showed the jury how sick Edward was in the opening statement, in the examinations of several witnesses, and in the closing argument.

We also reenacted significant scenes with Edward's wife and children to learn their stories, and how their stories contributed to the case story. We had them reenact scenes that reflected their love for Edward, and their greatest fears when he was sick. They all returned to the same scene – a scene of Edward in the hospital surrounded by his entire family with a pastor beside him. Edward lay there as a feeble, jaundiced man far older than his 58 years. When he took his daughter's hand and told her "I will be alright," she left the room to cry because she knew that her father was dying.

Of course, I didn't just do reenactments with the family. I did the usual lawyer things, like taking depositions. An extraordinary thing happened during the deposition of the medical director who denied Edward's request: He got up and walked out of his deposition. No, he stormed out. He projected anger. I had a gut feeling that he was ashamed. Coincidentally, he had also been a poor immigrant from the Middle East. I had his CV, of course, from which I learned that he started out providing primary care to poor people. By the time he denied Edward's transplant request, he had become a highly paid bureaucrat. To cross examine him successfully, I wanted to uncover the real feelings behind that anger. I used a role reversal to try to understand the medical director. In other words, like an actor studying for a role, I tried to assume his role to understand his feelings. Through the role reversal with the help of others, I gained insight into how this doctor abandoned his dreams of taking care of people.

Similarly, I reversed roles with the treating University doctor, whose superiors would not be happy about his referring a patient to another hospital for a transplant. And his superiors would not be happy about him testifying against a large, powerful insurance company that pays University tens of millions of dollars each year. In the role reversal I felt what it was like to spend your entire career studying and then working at one prestigious academic hospital. I cared about my career and being valued by my boss, the head of the transplant department at the university. I felt what it was like to be the sole provider for several young children and a stay-at-home wife. My greatest fear was to lose my position at the prestigious university medical center. So I met with the doctor early in the case, with my client, to build rapport based on truth. In the first session of his deposition the doctor testified truthfully, but in a very guarded fashion. But before the second session of his deposition, the University retained counsel for the doctor. And the doctor suddenly changed his testimony to help the insurer.

Through the role reversals and questions, the theme of caring became very apparent. The insurance company medical directors felt like bureaucratic automatons whose patient was the company. They did not care about the sick people who relied upon the company in their time of need. We learned that people were very critical of the university doctor for not documenting the referral to Texas in the medical records and not advocating for Edward.

Later, I convened a focus group. I used a "100 questions" method. This method involves the use of free association. For example, I read the word "liver transplant" and had them write down the first words that came into their mind. Tellingly, the jurors thought of alcoholism, the illegal purchase of human organs, and wealthy people moving to other states to "jump the line" and receive organs ahead of others on the local wait lists. This highlighted crucial issues that I needed to address when speaking to my jurors.

Trial

In this case, I started the case with the bad guys. I called three company medical directors who had denied the transplant or appeals to show the betrayal. The role reversals and scene setting helped me develop cross examinations for each witness.

The Court changed its pretrial rulings and allowed the defense to present evidence implying that Edward was a wealthy man who jumped the line ahead of other sick people to get a quicker transplant. Had we not devoted significant time to discovering the emotional core of Edward and his family's story, I don't know if we would have prevailed in the face of that defense. But that argument rang hollow when the jury got to hear from Edward and his family.

When it came time for the university physician to testify, he failed to show up at trial. Once we compelled his appearance, I didn't know whether he would testify truthfully or testify for the insurer – although I suspected that he would protect himself and testify for the insurer. So I tried to tell his story truthfully to show the jury why he was not supporting his own patient.

Ultimately, the jury found that the insurer acted in bad faith and unreasonably denied the transplant.

Chapter 32: Kaiser Autism Denials

Six years ago, Guillermo, a tall thin man with an unkempt beard and deep brown eyes, walked into my office. He was agitated and trembling as he told me that Kaiser Foundation Health Plan had refused to provide his two-year-old autistic son with Applied Behavioral Analysis ("ABA") – the most effective treatment for autism. Kaiser, a "not-for-profit" health plan, had also refused to provide his son with necessary speech therapy. Because early intervention is crucial for autistic children, Guillermo's desperation was palpable.

Autism Spectrum Disorders ("ASDs") are a group of developmental disorders which onset in early childhood and often cause significant social, communication, and behavioral challenges. Individuals with ASDs demonstrate varying degrees of deficits in social interaction, verbal and nonverbal communication, and repetitive behaviors or interests. There is no physiological test, like a blood test, to determine if someone has an ASD. Instead, doctors analyze a child's behavior and development to make a diagnosis.

While there is no cure for ASDs, ABA is widely accepted as the most effective treatment. ABA is a process of collecting data on an individual's behavior and using a variety of behavioral conditioning techniques to teach and reinforce desired behaviors while extinguishing harmful or undesired behaviors. Studies have repeatedly shown that ABA improves cognitive abilities and adaptive behavior, enabling numerous children to achieve "normalcy" and function in everyday life.

Kaiser, like every other health insurer in California, refused to provide ABA to its members with ASDs. Kaiser systematically denied ABA on the ground that it was not a medical service, was not provided by licensed medical providers, and was merely educational. In order to evade its obligation to provide coverage for the service, Kaiser claimed that ABA was a learning method that was primarily used in schools, and that it was provided directly to children through individuals with no medical training.

I took Guillermo's case, and others like it, and filed a class action against Kaiser to stop them from systematically denying ABA for children with ASDs.

When I started to work on the cases, I struggled to understand ASDs. Though defined above, it is difficult to understand what ASDs really are since their definition is amorphous. How can we tell the story of ASDs so people can wrap their arms around what autism truly is? What is the emotional core of the stories about children with autism that will make people care?

To start to discover the numerous stories involved in these cases, and answer the questions above, I began by reversing roles with a three-year-old, non-verbal autistic boy. I started to learn the story when I was spinning around in circles as a three-year-old boy without making any eye contact. To be totally disconnected from other human beings, in my own world, and unable to communicate was overwhelming. As the boy was non-verbal, we utilized the psychodramatic techniques of role reversals, doubling, and soliloquy. The role reversals had a powerful impact on all of us. I discovered how scary, confusing, and overwhelming each day must be for children with autism. In addition, I learned that reenactments were the only way to discover the emotional power of the story of an autistic child. Without understanding the tremendous limitations caused by ASDs, one cannot fully appreciate the importance of ABA.

I then reversed roles with parents of children with ASDs. I learned how incredibly difficult each day must be. I felt helpless and hopeless in being imprisoned by autism. I experienced fear, anger, hurt, resentment, helplessness, and hopelessness. For example, the fears I experienced included tremendous fears about my daughter's future. I also worried about being able to keep my job and support my family when my daughter requires my full-time, around the clock attention. I learned about how difficult every day must be caring for a child who cannot communicate, express her wants or needs, sleep, show affection, or even keep from physically hurting herself. Looking to the future, I was afraid of whether my daughter would ever talk, have friends, get married, be employed, or even be able to care for herself. I was infuriated that Kaiser would not cover the ABA that could help my daughter potentially fully recover from her autism.

After working on the sociodrama, I conducted reenactments with several parents. One courageous mother explored scenes revealing her infertility and related marital problems. Her drive to be a mother was powerful, and the birth of her son was the best day in her life. Her son was the center of her universe. We then explored the scene of her child being diagnosed with autism. We reenacted a powerful and depressing scene of her dropping her son off for the first time at a special preschool for children with severe disabilities. These scenes, witnessed through powerful doubling, led us to discover her pain. But more importantly, these scenes led us to understand the incredible love she has for her son and the power of her caring. We learned that she would fight for her son, against anything (including a massive insurance company), to give her son the best life possible. We discovered the story of this mother's love.

To further discover the story, I spent time with my autistic clients. I began by spending time at a child named Billy's house. Having two young kids, I was familiar with the normal stressors involved. However, I was completely overwhelmed with the chaos, stress, and lack of control in his house. Billy spun in circles in the living room as his family repeatedly tried to stop him from injuring himself – but Billy still persisted. As Billy rarely slept for more than a few hours at a time, his entire family seemed overwhelmed, sleep-deprived, beaten down, defeated, and helpless. Normal daily activities, such as feeding, bathing, and dressing, were difficult and time-consuming. I learned that getting through each day with an autistic child requires tremendous strength, courage, and perseverance. It was obvious that families with an autistic child are incredibly overwhelmed. As a result, these families rarely have the strength and fortitude to mount a battle against a powerful insurance company to fight for ABA. At the same time, I became empowered with the realization that helping one child get ABA could change the lives of his or her entire family.

I next spent an evening babysitting a 12-year-old, high-functioning child with autism named Rick. Thanks to substantial early ABA intervention that his family paid for privately, he has no trouble communicating. In fact, unless you were very knowledgeable about autism, you would not realize that there is anything unusual about him. He had many photographs on the wall in his bedroom. We spent time reenacting the events that were depicted in the photographs. It was inspiring to learn about his life, his loves, and his fears.

I also reversed roles with a Kaiser primary care physician. I explored how difficult it must be for a doctor, who wants to help patients, to be unable to help patients with the most effective autism treatment. I learned how powerless it must feel to be a Kaiser doctor, who in many ways is just a cog in the Kaiser machine.

I also gained insight by contemplating Kaiser's main defenses. For example, Kaiser claimed that ABA is not a medical service. I was able to explore peoples' thoughts about what constitutes a medical service. I learned that our trial presentation must be filled with physicians' testimony and numerous medical feeling visuals such as MRI reports, genetic testing reports, PET scans, and other scientific visuals to reinforce that ABA is a medical service.

After almost six years of work, Kaiser finally agreed to change their policies and stop systematically denying ABA and speech therapy to children with ASDs. As part of the settlement, it has established a large fund to reimburse families that paid for ABA and speech therapy over the past eight years. In addition, the fund provided money for cutting-edge autism research at UCLA and UCSF.

SECTION VIII: BARRIERS TO RECOVERY – ERISA AND FIGTHING ARBITRATION

Chapter 33: ERISA Preemption

Private employer sponsored health plans are unique in that they are governed by a federal law known as the Employee Retirement Income Security Act of 1974 ("ERISA"). Although the reach of ERISA preemption is a complicated subject, in general, if the client has health insurance through an employer, and is not self-employed or employed by the government or a religious organization, ERISA probably preempts the claims.[101] This law limits what a covered insured can recover. Under ERISA, an insured cannot recover for anything other than the cost of the treatment and potentially some attorneys' fees.[102] Specifically, ERISA policy holders cannot seek consequential damages, emotional distress damages or punitive damages.[103] When suing for a wrongful denial, an attorney can seek to recover attorneys' fees regardless of whether the insured's policy is an ERISA policy or an individual policy.

In addition to different damages, the procedure for suing under an ERISA policy differs from the procedure for suing under an individual policy. For example, a claimant does not have the right to a jury trial in ERISA-preempted actions because the remedies available to a participant or beneficiary under ERISA are equitable in nature while a claimant who brings an action under a non-ERISA case has a right to a jury trial.[104] Under ERISA, plans must provide reasonable claims procedures and allow a fair review of claims that the insurance companies denied. ERISA plans will include a description of the internal appeals process in a summary of the plan which they will provide to the policyholder. Among other ERISA requirements, the whole process must not require more than two levels of internal appeals before the claimant may file an action in court, and the claimant's right to sue cannot be eliminated (for example, the plan cannot require binding arbitration).

Further, before a group health plan can deny an appeal based on a new or additional reason than what the plan used in their formal denial, it must provide to the consumer free of charge and as soon as possible information about the new or additional rationale and the evidence supporting it. This rule was made so that the insured can have all of the relevant information and evidence before the appeal is decided so that the insured can be prepared to dispute the evidence supporting the denial. It is important to remember that ERISA requires appeals to be filed within 180 days after denial, but the specific plan might have additional time deadlines.

Insureds have a right to challenge the denial of a claim for coverage in a court of law. Whether the insured's policy is subject to ERISA affects the way a consumer can challenge the wrongful conduct of an insurer. As explained above, policies purchased through an employer (with certain exceptions) are subject to ERISA while individual policies generally are not. The non-individual policies not subject to ERISA are: plans for employees of the government and public agencies; plans for employees of churches or church-operated businesses, unless the employer properly elected to fall under ERISA; and policies issued to sole proprietors, partners, and their spouses, so long as the business does not provide benefits to any common-law employees.[105]

Chapter 34: Fighting Arbitration

Both federal and state laws favor the resolution of disputes through arbitration because arbitration is theoretically fast, fair and cheap. But in reality arbitration is often slow, unfair and expensive. This chapter addresses the framework within which consumer attorneys can fight mandatory, pre-dispute arbitration agreements in employment, consumer and managed-care contracts.

In analyzing arbitration clauses, courts generally address three questions. First, is the arbitration provision in a valid agreement? Second, is the arbitration clause unconscionable? And third, should the court enforce the arbitration agreement and simply sever the improper components of the arbitration agreement?

As the Supreme Court of the United States remarked, "Arbitration is a matter of contract and a party cannot be required to submit to arbitration any dispute which he has not agreed so to submit."[106] For this reason, the existence of an arbitration agreement is determined under standard rules of contract interpretation.[107] Similarly, defenses to contract of illusory agreement, fraud, duress, and lack of capacity equally apply to arbitration provisions as they do to contracts generally. If you have a factual scenario to match one of these defenses, then they can be very effective methods to attack an arbitration agreement.

In *Saika v. Gold* (1996) 49 Cal.App.4th 1074, the Court of Appeal examined an illusory and thus unenforceable agreement. Specifically, the arbitration agreement at issue had a provision that permitted either of the parties subject to the agreement, a doctor and his patient, to reject any award resulting from arbitration of $25,000 or greater and in such a case request a trial judge in superior court hear the case de novo.[108] The Court of Appeal explained its decision by stating that as "a practical matter, the benefit which the trial de novo clause confers on patients is nothing more than a chimera. The odds that an award will both (a) clear the $25,000 threshold but (b) still be so low that the patient would want to have a trial de novo are so small as to be negligible. Unless we are to assume that arbitrators in medical malpractice cases regularly and capriciously make awards substantially below what justice requires—and that is an assumption which we will not indulge the cases where the trial de novo clause could possibly benefit the patient are going to be rare indeed."[109] The court concluded that "the rejection clause meant the arbitration agreement really did not function as an arbitration agreement. The promise of an inexpensive, speedy resolution to the claim evaporated with one party's unilateral ability to avoid results it did not like. "[110]

Illusory arbitration agreements are often found in long term service contracts or employment handbooks. Such arbitration agreements usually result from inclusions in the agreements that one of the parties can unilaterally modify the terms of the arbitration agreement at will. An example of such an agreement is found in *Sparks v. Vista Del Mar Child & Family Services* (2012) 207 Cal.App.4th 1511, 1523, a case in which the court was determining whether to enforce an arbitration agreement in an employee handbook and held that an "agreement to arbitrate is illusory if, as here, the employer can unilaterally modify the handbook."[111] One point of caution though is found in the fact that the California Supreme Court has not directly addressed such an argument and another division of the California Court of Appeal in *Serpa v. California Surety Investigations, Inc.* (2013) 215 Cal.App.4th 695 described the above quoted language as mere dicta.[112]

Courts can find that parties did not enter into a contract not just because the contract is illusory but also because the contract is the result of fraud. California law distinguishes between two types of fraudulent contracts: fraud in the "execution" or "inception" of a contract and fraud in the "inducement" of a contract. In the former case "the fraud goes to the inception or execution of the agreement, so that the promisor is deceived as to the nature of his act, and actually does not know what he is signing, or does not intend to enter into a contract at all, mutual assent is lacking, and [the contract] is void. In such a case it may be disregarded without the necessity of rescission."[113] Fraud in the inducement, by contrast, occurs when "the promisor knows what he is signing but his consent is induced by fraud, mutual assent is present and a contract is formed, which, by reason of the fraud, is voidable. In order to escape from its obligations, the aggrieved party must rescind. . . ."[114]

Where "a party's apparent assent to a written contract is *negated* by fraud in the inception, there is simply no arbitration agreement to be enforced."[115] In other words, if a plaintiff can make a showing of fraud in the execution of an agreement, then that plaintiff can avoid a motion to compel arbitration. "By contrast, a claim that a contract containing an arbitration clause is unenforceable because of fraud in the inducement of a contract as a whole is for the arbitrator and not the court to decide (because such a fraud would make the contract voidable but not void)."[116]

These approaches illustrate a practitioner's first method of attacking an arbitration agreement and equally apply whether the arbitration agreement arose in the context of an employment, consumer, or managed health care action. All of these approaches concern the basic question of whether the parties actually assented to arbitration in a valid and enforceable manner.

Is the Arbitration Agreement Unconscionable?

All arbitration agreements must be conscionable.[117] Unconscionability has procedural and substantive components and both components must be present for a court to refuse to enforce an arbitration provision based on unconscionability. But the elements need not be present in the same degree. Courts use a sliding scale approach in evaluating the two elements. The more substantively unconscionable the agreement is, the less procedural unconscionability is necessary. The more procedurally unconscionable an agreement is, the less substantive unconscionability is necessary.

Procedural unconscionability involves the manner in which an agreement was negotiated. The key issues are oppression and surprise. Oppression derives from an inequality of bargaining power of the parties and an absence of real negotiation or meaningful choice on the part of the weaker party. Surprise arises when a challenged term is hidden in a printed form drafted by the party seeking to enforce the arbitration provision. When an adhesion contract is oppressive, no surprise is necessary.[118] Adhesion contracts that are offered on a take it or leave it basis are procedurally unconscionable.[119]

Substantive unconscionability addresses whether the terms of an agreement are overly harsh or so one-sided as to "shock the conscience." Most importantly, an agreement must involve mutuality. When only the weaker party's claims are subject to arbitration, and there is no reasonable justification for the lack of symmetry, the agreement lacks the requisite degree of mutuality.[120] Courts have identified a number of factors that may result in substantive unconscionability including, but not limited to:

1. lack of mutuality without justification;
2. imposition of improper arbitration fees;
3. limitation on potential remedies;
4. prohibiting or *severely* restricting discovery;
5. contractual limitations provisions that are shorter than applicable statutes of limitations;
6. requiring arbitrations to remain confidential; and
7. requirements regarding the location of an arbitration;

For example, several courts have determined that arbitration agreements that require fee-splitting are substantively unconscionable.[121]

Similarly, several courts have found that prohibiting or severely restricting discovery is substantively unconscionable. *Armendariz* provided that claimants are entitled to discovery sufficient to adequately arbitrate their statutory claims, including access to essential documents and witnesses.[122] Adequate discovery is not synonymous with unfettered discovery, but because discovery limitations are often advantageous to the party seeking arbitration, they can be substantively unconscionable.[123] California cases have not specified how much an arbitration agreement can limit discovery without rendering the agreement substantively unconscionable.[124]

Courts have also found that arbitration agreements

requiring arbitrations to be confidential can be substantively unconscionable.[125] In *Ting*, the court reasoned that confidentiality provisions favor companies over individuals because companies are "repeat players" in the arbitration process. Normally, plaintiffs' attorneys and arbitration companies such as the American Arbitration Association can evaluate arbitration awards and develop a body of knowledge about a company to mitigate the company's advantage of being a repeat player. But confidentiality provisions can stop a company's opponents from reviewing past arbitration awards and developing information necessary to build a case of intentional misconduct or unlawful discrimination.[126]

The Unconscionability Approach Survives in a Post-*AT&T v. Concepcion* World

The Supreme Court of the United States changed the landscape of defenses to motions to compel arbitration when it decided *AT&T v. Concepcion* (2011) 131 S.Ct. 1740 (*Concepcion*) and there has been a lot of confusion as to whether the ruling completely invalidated all state law defenses to arbitration agreements but as the California Supreme Court recently pointed out, *Concepcion* did not wholly alter existing defenses in such a dramatic fashion.[127] In fact, *Concepcion* reaffirmed that the Federal Arbitration Act (FAA) "permits arbitration agreements to be declared unenforceable 'upon such grounds as exist at law or in equity for the revocation of any contract'"[128], including "generally applicable contract defenses, such as fraud, duress, or unconscionability."[129]

Subsequently, the California Supreme Court specifically addressed the defense of unconscionability by unequivocally declaring that "[a]fter *Concepcion*, courts may continue to apply unconscionability doctrine to arbitration agreements."[130] However, courts may not indiscriminately apply the unconscionability doctrine as they once had. The California

Supreme Court explained that "state courts may continue to enforce unconscionability rules that do not 'interfere[ ] with fundamental attributes of arbitration.'"[131] "*Concepcion* clarifies the limits the FAA places on state unconscionability rules as they pertain to arbitration agreements. It is well-established that such rules must not facially discriminate against arbitration and must be enforced evenhandedly. *Concepcion* goes further to make clear that such rules, even when facially nondiscriminatory, must not disfavor arbitration as applied by imposing procedural requirements that "interfere[ ] with fundamental attributes of arbitration," especially its " 'lower costs, greater efficiency and speed, and the ability to choose expert adjudicators to resolve specialized disputes.' [Citation.]"[132] Importantly, state law rules that do not "interfere[ ] with fundamental attributes of arbitration" do not implicate *Concepcion*'s limits on state unconscionability rules.[133]

The California Supreme Court recently reiterated the viability of unconscionability rules by explicitly stating that *Conception* "does not limit the unconscionability rules applicable to other provisions of the arbitration agreement."[134] The Court again explained that the rules of unconscionability are equally applied to arbitration and non-arbitration agreements and so remains a valid defense to a petition to compel arbitration.[135]

Avoid the "Unwaivable Right" Defense to Arbitration and Class Action Waivers

A traditional defense to arbitration agreements that courts sometimes treat as a type of unconscionability defense but in other times treat as distinct defenses are defenses based on the fact that arbitration agreement provisions implicate unwaivable public rights, either based in public policy or California statute.[136] It is important to understand this rule as it was widely used in consumer lawsuits in the past but it is no longer a viable defense to arbitration in the bad faith context.

In *Broughton v. Cigna Healthplans* (1999) 21 Cal.4th 1066, 1082–1084 the Court held that claims for injunctive relief under the CLRA were not subject to arbitration. In a similar case, *Cruz v. PacifiCare* (2003) 30 Cal.4th 303, a health plan member sued his health plan for unfair competition and false advertising under the Consumer Legal Remedies Act ("CLRA") and Business and Professions Code sections 17200 and 17500. The court extended the *Broughton* rule and held that injunctive relief claims under the CLRA and Business and Professions Code section 17200 are not arbitrable since they are designed to benefit the public. Subsequent courts refer to the rule that causes of action for injunctive relief under the CLRA are not subject to arbitration agreements as the *Broughton-Cruz* rule.

As it stands today, the validity of the *Broughton-Cruz* doctrine is in serious doubt. The California Supreme Court has not generated a holding that directly addresses the survival of this rule post-*Concepcion.* This being said, the Court of Appeal has subsequently held that the *Broughton-Cruz* doctrine is preempted by federal law pursuant to the Supreme Court of the United States' decision in *Concepcion.*[137] The California Supreme Court did grant review of this decision in April of 2015 but there is no present indication as to how the Court will rule.

If the California Supreme Court looks to federal courts, then it will likely uphold the finding of preemption. In a recent decision, the Ninth Circuit Court of Appeals also held that federal law preempts the *Broughton-Cruz* rule since the rule improperly restricts a certain type of claim from arbitration.[138] The Ninth Circuit Court of Appeals had originally came to a similar conclusion in *Kilgore v. KeyBank, Nat. Assn.* (9th Cir.2012) 673 F.3d 947 but subsequently reheard the case en banc and decided it on narrower grounds, deciding to not reach the question of whether *Broughton-Cruz* survives *Concepcion.*[139]

The Gentry Rule and Classwide Arbitration Limitations

Another historically substantial defense to arbitration based upon unwaivable public rights related to class action waivers and the *Gentry* rule. In *Gentry v. Sup.Ct. (Circuit City Stores, Inc.)* (2007) 42 Cal.4th 443, the court held that arbitration agreements in the employment context in which an employee waives their right to bring class claims in arbitration are unenforceable when class wide arbitration is a more effective practical means of vindicating employee rights due to "the modest size of the potential individual recovery"; "the potential for retaliation against members of the class"; "the fact that absent members of the class may be ill informed about their rights"; and "other real world obstacles to the vindication of class members' right to overtime pay through individual arbitration."[140] The *Gentry* court did not base their holding on an unconscionability argument but instead concerned "the effect of a class action waiver on unwaivable statutory rights regardless of unconscionability."[141]

At least one California Court has previously held that the *Gentry* rule survived *Concepcion.*[142] However, the California Supreme recently weighed in on the subject and ruled that federal law does in fact preempt the *Gentry* rule with only very narrow exception for certain employment cases based upon California's Private Attorney General Act.[143] The result is that class action waivers are currently enforceable in arbitration agreements in the insurance context.

Is the Arbitration Agreement in Clear and Understandable Language?

If the arbitration agreement is found within the healthcare service plan, then it is subject to additional statutory rules that can also provide a defense to a motion to compel arbitration. Specifically, Health & Safety Code § 1369.1 requires that:

> Any health care service plan that includes terms that require binding arbitration to settle disputes and that restrict, or provide for a waiver of, the right to a jury trial shall include, in **clear and understandable language**, a disclosure that meets all of the following conditions:
>
> (a) The disclosure shall clearly state whether the plan uses binding arbitration to settle disputes, including specifically whether the plan uses binding arbitration to settle claims of medical malpractice.
> (b) The disclosure shall appear as a separate article in the agreement issued to the employer group or individual subscriber and **shall be prominently displayed** on the enrollment form signed by each subscriber or enrollee.
> (c) The disclosure **shall clearly state whether the subscriber or enrollee is waiving his or her right to a jury trial** for medical malpractice, other disputes relating to the delivery of service under the plan, or both, and shall be substantially expressed in the wording provided in subdivision (a) of Section 1295 of the Code of Civil Procedure.
> (d) In any contract or enrollment agreement for a health care service plan, the disclosure required by this section shall be displayed immediately before the signature line provided for the representative of the group contracting with a health care service plan and immediately before the signature line provided for the individual enrolling in the health care service plan. (Emphasis added.)

Although the three bolded requirements are not the only requirements for an arbitration agreement by the code provision, they are very important provision for which a violation of each can invalidate an arbitration agreement.

A health care plan's failure to comply with the disclosure requirements of Health & Safety Code § 1363.1 renders an arbitration clause unenforceable.[144] Section 1363.1 "clearly indicates an individual who enrolls in a health care service plan will receive a certain type of disclosure which is prominently displayed immediately before the signature line on the form the individual signs to enroll in the plan."[145] Absent this disclosure and signature, there can be no enforceable arbitration clause.[146]

In *Medeiros v. Sup. Ct.* (2007) 146 Cal.App.4th 1008, 1017, Health Net brought a motion to compel arbitration and the trial court granted the motion. On appeal, Health Net argued that § 1363.1's disclosure requirements applied only to the group service agreement between it and the County of San Bernardino, plaintiff Medeiros's employer, and that "Medeiros [was] bound by the arbitration provisions found in the group service application and group service agreement between Health Net and the County . . . ."[147] Health Net also argued that the benefits election form signed by Medeiros provided actual notice of the arbitration provision contained in the evidence of coverage.[148] The court of appeal rejected each of Health Net's arguments, and entered a peremptory writ of mandate directing the trial court to vacate its order compelling arbitration.[149] The appellate court's holding that § 1363.1's disclosure requirements were "mandatory" was based on its review of an unbroken string of appellate court decisions that have "'concluded that strict compliance with section 1363.1 is required to enforce [an] arbitration provision' in a health service plan."[150]

In *Burks v. Kaiser Foundation Health Plan, Inc.* (2008) 160 Cal.App.4th 1021, the court of appeal held that an arbitration clause in a managed health care service plan failed to satisfy §1363.1's disclosure requirements and was unenforceable because the notice was not "prominently displayed." Despite that the arbitration clause in *Burks* was the only text on the form[151] and was located immediately above the signature line[152], the court held that it was "not prominently displayed" given "the plain, small typeface Kaiser used for its arbitration disclosure without any heading, and given that most of the rest of the form . . . contains larger typeface, some of which is bold and some of which is highlighted by a different colored background. . ."[153]

The court reached a similar conclusion In *Robertson v. Health Net of California, Inc.* in which the court found a separate arbitration agreement to fail to meet the disclosure. Specifically, it found that "(1) the [arbitration] provision is some distance from the enrollees' signature line, (2) the provision is printed in the same font or typeface as the rest of the form, and (3) only the title is in bolded type," and so it concluded that the arbitration clause failed to meet the mandatory "prominen[ce]" requirement of section 1363.1, subdivision (b).[154]

Severing Illegal or Unconscionable Provisions of Arbitration Agreements

Courts may enforce arbitration agreements that are improper if the improper terms can be severed. This reflects a policy to prevent parties from gaining an undeserved benefit or suffering an undeserved detriment from voiding the entire agreement. Severance also attempts to maintain a contractual relationship if to do so would not condone an illegal scheme.[155] The main issue is whether severance serves the interests of justice.[156]

Courts have identified several factors that affect severability. First, courts generally will void an arbitration agreement and not sever improper provisions when the "good cannot be separated from the bad, or rather the bad enters into and permeates the whole contract, so that none of it can be said to be good."[157]

Second, courts examine the contract's main purpose. If the central purpose of the contract is tainted with illegality, courts cannot enforce the contract. But if the illegality is collateral to the main purpose of the contract, and the illegal provision can be removed from the contract through severance or restriction, then courts will enforce the contract and sever or restrict the improper provisions.[158]

Third, courts evaluate whether the agreement contains more than one objectionable term to measure the pervasiveness of a contract's illegality or unconscionability.[159] If an arbitration agreement contains more than one improper term, it may reflect a systematic effort to impose arbitration on an employee as an inferior forum that advantages the employer and may justify the conclusion that the arbitration agreement is permeated with an unlawful purpose.[160]

Similarly, courts will find a contract permeated by illegality or unconscionability where there is no single provision that the court can strike or restrict in order to remove the unconscionability from the agreement.[161] Courts have no power to cure illegality by reformation. The court can only cure a contract's illegality through severance or restriction. If the court cannot remove the taint of illegality through reformation, the court cannot enforce the arbitration provision.[162]

ABOUT THE AUTHOR

Scott Glovsky is an attorney in Los Angeles who focuses on health insurance bad faith and trial work. He appeared in the film *SiCKO* and *People Magazine*, and his cases have been profiled on CNN and other major networks. Mr. Glovsky recently litigated *Arce v. Kaiser Foundation Health Plan* on behalf of over 45,000 autistic children. The lawsuit resulted in Kaiser stopping its systemic denials of speech therapy and applied behavioral analysis for autistic children. Mr. Glovsky has received numerous awards including *California Lawyer Magazine's* California Lawyer Attorney of the Year Award and the Consumer Attorneys of California's Street Fighter of the Year Award. Scott frequently lectures and writes in the area of health insurance law, and is an instructor at Gerry Spence's Trial Lawyers College. Mr. Glovsky received his undergraduate degree from the University of California, Berkeley and his J.D. from Cornell Law School. Scott can be reached at www.scottglovsky.com.

NOTES

[1] In this book I use the terms associated with health insurers and managed health care plans interchangeably because generally the same law applies. For example, "health insurer" is synonymous with "managed care plan" and "insured" is interchangeable with "subscriber." Exceptions are noted.

[2] Code Civ. Proc. § 425.10(a)(1)

[3] *Id.* at 415

[4] *Davaloo, supra*, 135 Cal.App.4th at 417

[5] *Id.* at 419

[6] *Id.* at 417

7 See, e.g., *Progressive West Ins. Co. v. Yolo County Superior Court* (2005) 135 Cal.App.4th 263, 278 (37 Cal.Rptr.3d 434)

[8] *Shade Foods, Inc. v. Innovative Products Sales & Marketing, Inc.* (2000) 78 Cal.App.4th 847, 890 (3 Cal.Rptr.2d 364) internal

quotations and brackets omitted

[9] *State Farm Fire & Casualty Co. v. Superior Court (Allegro)* (1996) 45 Cal.App.4th 1093 (53 Cal.Rptr.2d 229), but see, *Textron Financial Corp. v. National Union Fire Ins. Co. of Pittsburgh* (2004) 118 Cal.App.4th 1061, 1072 [3 Cal.Rptr.3d 586], which suggests (erroneously in the author's view) that *Allegro* is no longer good law in light of *Cel-Tech Communications, Inc. v. Los Angeles Cellular Telephone Co.* (1999) 20 Cal.4th 163 (83 Cal.Rptr.2d 548)

[10] *Moore v. American United Life Insurance Company*, supra, 150 Cal.App.3d at p. 640 (197 Cal.Rptr. at 897)

[11] 509 U.S. at 462, emphasis added

[12] 419 S.E.2d at 881

[13] 419 S.E.2d at 882

[14] 419 S.E.2d 882

[15] 419 S.E.2d at 882, 883

[16] 419 S.E.2d at 883

[17] 419 S.E.2d at 885, 886

[18] CCP § 437c(b)(1)

[19] Black's Law Dictionary (9th ed. 2009), voir dire

[20] CCP § 208

[21] CCP § 219(a)

[22] CCP § 220

[23] CCP § 222(a)

[24] CCP § 222.5; CRC 3.1540(b)

[25] CCP § 222.5

[26] FRCP 47(a); FRCP 47(a); see *Csiszer v. Wren*, supra, 614 F3d at 875; *Alcala v. Embhart Indus.*, Inc. (7th Cir. 2007) 495 F3d 360, 363

[27] FRCP 47(a); FRCP 47(a); see *Csiszer v. Wren*, supra, 614 F3d at 875; *Alcala v. Embhart Indus.*, Inc. (7th Cir. 2007) 495 F3d 360, 363

[28] See *Skilling v. United States* (2010) 130 S.Ct. 2896, 2919

[29] CCP § 222.5

[30] CCP § 222.5

[31] CCP § 222.5

---

[32] See *People v. Williams* (1981) 29 Cal.3d 392, 402 (superseded by statute and constitutional amendment on other grounds)
[33] See *People v. Ah Lee Doon* (1893) 97 Cal. 171, 179; *Kramm v. Stockton Elec. R.R. Co.* (1913) 22 Cal.App. 737, 746–747
[34] CCP § 222.5
[35] CCP § 222.5
[36] CCP § 222.5; CRC 3.1540(d)
[37] CRC 3.1549
[38] CCP § 222.5; see *Bellas v. Sup.Ct. (People)* (2000) 85 Cal.App.4th 636, 639
[39] CCP § 222.5
[40] See *People v. Tolbert* (1969) 70 Cal.2d 790, 812
[41] *People v. Williams* (1981) 29 Cal.3d 392, 410
[42] *In re Malvasi's Estate* (1929) 96
[43] *In re Malvasi's Estate*, supra, 96 CA at 210
[44] See *Bohme v. Southern Pac. Co.* (1970) 8 Cal.App.3d 291, 296–297 (disapproved on other grounds in *Lund v. San Joaquin Valley* R.R. (2003) 31 Cal.4th 1, 11); See *Tellefsen v. Key System Transit Lines* (1958) 158 Cal.App.2d 243, 246–247; Ev. C. § 1152
[45] *People v. Williams*, supra, 29 Cal.3d at 408
[46] CCP § 222.5
[47] *Richmond v. Moore* (1930) 103 Cal.App 173, 178
[48] *Bly-Magee v. Budget Rent-A-Car Corp.* (1994) 24 Cal.App.4th 318, 324
[49] Local Rule 3.48(c) and (d)
[50] Local Rule 3.50
[51] Black's Law Dictionary (9th ed. 2009), opening statement
[52] Black's Law Dictionary (9th ed. 2009), opening statement
[53] *People v. Arnold* (1926) 199 Cal. 471, 486
[54] CCP § 607
[55] CRC 2.1034
[56] CCP § 607(1)
[57] CCP § 607(2)
[58] CCP § 607
[59] CCP § 607(8)

---

[60] CCP § 631.7
[61] *Rosenfield v. Vosper* (1948) 86 Cal.App.2d 687
[62] CRC 3.1550
[63] *Williams v. Goodman* (1963) 214 Cal.App.2d 856, 869; *Winfred D. v. Michelin North America, Inc.* (2008) 165 Cal.App.4th 1011, 1027–1028
[64] *U.S. v. Magallanez* (10th Cir.2005) 408 F.3d 672, 678, *U.S. v. Segal* (9th Cir.1988) 852 F.2d 1152, 1155–1156; *U.S. v. Chavez* (10th Cir.2000) 229 F.3d 946, 952
[65] *De Armas v. Dickerman* (1952) 108 Cal.App.2d 548, 553
[66] *Hawk v. Sup.Ct. (People)* (1974) 42 Cal.App.3d 108, 121
[67] *Smith v. Covell* (1980) 100 Cal.App.3d 947, 958; Ev. C. § 350
[68] *Hawk v. Sup.Ct. (People)* (1974) 42 Cal.App.3d 108, 118
[69] *Mudrick v. Market St. Ry. Co.* (1938) 11 Cal.2d 724, 737; *Smith v. Covell* (1980) 100 Cal.App.3d 947, 958; *People v. Bolton* (1979) 23 Cal.3d 208, 214; *Love v. Wolf* (1964) 226 Cal.App.2d 378, 392–394
[70] LASC Local Rule 3.97
[71] LASC Local Rule 3.97
[72] CCP § 581c(a)
[73]See *Nuffer v. Insurance Co. of North America* (1965) 236 Cal.App.2d 349, 362
[74] *Panico v. Truck Ins. Exchange* (2001) 90 Cal.App.4th 1294, 1299, 109 CR2d 638, 642; see *John Norton Farms v. Todagco* (1981) 124 Cal.App.3d 149, 161
[75] See *Jensen v. Hewlett–Packard Co.* (1993) 14 Cal.App.4th 958, 969–970
[76] *State Farm Mut. Auto. Ins. Co. v. Campbell, et. al.*, 123 S.Ct. 1513 (2003)
[77] See Civ. Code §3302; *Howard v. American Nat'l fire Ins. Co.* 187 Cal. App. 4th 498, 537 (2010)
[78] *Frazier v. Metropolitan Life Ins. Co.* 169 Cal. 3d 90 (1985).
[79] See *Jonathan Neil & Asoc., Inc. v. Jones* (2004) 33 Cal. 4th 917.
[80] *Crisci v. Security Ins. Co. of New Haven, Conn.* 66 Cal.2d 425, 433, 58 Cal.Rptr 13, 18 (1967)

---

[81] *Waters v. United Services Auto Assn*, 41 Cal.App.4th 1063, 1079, 48 Cal.Rptr.2d 910, 920 (1996)
[82] *Cassim v. Allstate Ins. Co.*, 33 Cal.4th 780, 16 Cal.Rptr.3d 374, 392 (2006)
[83] *Cassim v. Allstate Ins. Co.*, 33 Cal.4th 780, 16 Cal.Rptr.3d 374, 392 (2006)
[84] Crosky, Heesman Popik & Imre, California Practice Guide: Insurance Litigation (Rutter 2012) ¶ 13:527
[85] Crosky, Heesman Popik & Imre, California Practice Guide: Insurance Litigation (Rutter 2011) ¶ 13:403
[86] See *Sumpter v. Matteson*, 158 Cal. App. 4th 928, 936 (2008); *Spinks v. Equity Residential Briarwood Apts.*, 171 Cal. App. 4th 1004, 1052 (2009)
[87] The "big 3" cases on punitive damages from the U.S. Supreme Court that you must look to are: *BMW v. Gore*, 517 U.S. 559, 116 S. Ct. 1589, 134 L. Ed. 2d 809 (1996), *State Farm Mut. Auto. Ins. Co. v. Campbell*, 123 S. Ct. 1513 (2003); and *Philip Morris v. Williams*, 127 S.Ct. 1057 (2007). But there are other important cases you should read, think about and utilize. They include: *Johnson v. Ford Motor Co.* (2005) 35 Cal.4th 1191, *Simon v. San Paolo U.S. Holding Co.* (2005) 35 Cal.4th 379 *Campbell v. State Farm* (Utah 2004) 98 P.3d 409 [this is the Utah Supreme Court's decision after remand from the U.S. Supreme Court] In re Exxon Valdez (D. Alaska 2004) 296 F.Supp.2d 1071 [for jury instructions only]
[88] *Roby v. McKesson Corp.*, 47 Cal. 4th 686, 693 (2009) (given "relatively low degree of reprehensibility" of defendant's acts and the "substantial compensatory damages verdict, which included a substantial award of non-economic damages" a 1:1 ratio of compensatory to punitive damages was the maximum constitutionally permissible punitive damages award.)
[89]See, e.g., *Colonial Life Ins. Co. V. Superior Court*, 31 Cal.3d 785, 183 Cal.Rptr. 810 (1982); *Moore v. American United Ins. Co.*, 150 Cal.App.3d 610, 197 (1984)
[90] Health & Safety Code § 1341
[91] *Williams v. California Physicians' Service*, 72 Ca.App.4th 722,

729, 85 Cal.Rptr.2d 497 (1999)
[92] Health & Safety Code § 1348.6
[93] *Wilson v. Blue Cross of Southern California*, 222 Cal.App.3rd 660, 673 (1990)
[94] *Moore v. Regents of the Univ. of California*, 51 Cal.3d 120, 128-32, 148 Cal.Rptr.146, 149-52 (1990)
[95] *Egan v. Mutual of Omaha Ins. Co.*, 24 Cal.3d 809, 819, 169 Cal.Rptr.691, 696 (1979)
[96] Health & Safety Code § 1367.01(h)(4)
[97] Health & Safety Code § 1367(d)
[98] Health & Safety Code § 1367(d)
[99] *Grant v. Weatherholt,* 123 Cal.App.2d 34, 45, 266 P.2d 185, 186 (1954)
[100] Edward Nome's name has been changed to protect his privacy.
[101] 29 U.S.C. 1003(b) and 29 C.F.R. § 2510.3-3(b)
[102] *Massachusetts Mut. Life Ins. Co. v. Russell*, 473 U.S. 134
[103] *Massachusetts Mut. Life Ins. Co. v. Russell* (1985) 473 U.S. 134, 142-144; *Mertens v. Hewitt Assoc.* (1993) 508 U.S. 248, 255-259, 262-263
[104] *Thomas v. Oregon Fruit Products Co.* (9th Cir. 2000) 228 F.3d 991, 997
[105] (29 U.S.C. § 1003(b)(1), (2); 29 C.F.R. § 2510.3- 3(b), (c)(1), (c)(2)
[106]*United Steelworkers of America v. Warrior & Gulf Navigation Co.* (1960) 363 U.S. 574, 582
[107] .See *Badie v. Bank of America* (1998) 67 Cal.App.4th 779, 787; *Mitchell v. American Fair Credit Ass'n, Inc.* (2002) 99 Cal.App.4th 1345, 1355–1356
[108] *Id.* at 1080
[109] *Id.*
[110] *Id.* at 1081
[111] *Id.* at 1523
[112] *Id.* at 708 n. 7
[113] *Ford v. Shearson Lehman American Express, Inc.* (1986) 180 Cal.App.3d 1011, 1028

[114] *Id.*
[115] *Rosenthal v. Great Western Fin'l Securities Corp.* (1996) 14 Cal.4th 394, 416 (emphasis in original)
[116] *Id.* at 432
[117] *Armendariz v. Foundation Health Psychare Services, Inc.* (2000) 24 Cal.4th 83, 124
[118] *Abramson v. Juniper Networks, Inc.* (2004) 115 Cal.App.4th 638
[119] *Martinez v. Master Protection Corporation* (2004) 118 Cal.App.4th 107; *Abramson v. Juniper Networks, Inc., supra,* at page 656
[120] *Armendariz* at 119-120
[121] *Abramsom v. Juniper Networks, Inc.*, supra, 115 Cal.App.4th 638; *Martinez v. Master Protection Corporation, supra,* 118 Cal.App.4th 107; *O'Hare v. Municipal Resource Consultant* (2003) 107 Cal.App.4th 267; *Gutierrez v. Autowest, Inc.* (2003) 114 Cal.App.4th 77
[122] *Armendariz v. Foundation Health Psychare Services, Inc.*, supra, 24 Cal.4th 83 at 106
[123] *Martinez v. Master Protection Corporation, supra,* 118 Cal.App.4th 107; *McManus v. CIBC World Markets Corp.* (2003) 109 Cal.App.4th 76
[124] *Id.*
[125] *Ting v. AT&T, supra,* 319 F.3d 1126, 1151-52
[126] *Id.* at 1152; see also *Davis v. O'Melveny & Myers* (9th Cir.2007) 485 F.3d 1066 (overruled on another point in *Kilgore v. KeyBank, Nat. Ass'n* (9th Cir. 2012) 673 F.3d 947); *Pokorny v. Quixtar, Inc.* (9th Cir. 2010) 601 F.3d 987.)
[127] *Sonic-Calabasas A, Inc. v. Moreno* (2013) 57 Cal.4th 1109, 1139 cert. denied, (2014) 134 S.Ct. 2724
[128] *Concepcion*, *supra,* 131 S.Ct. at 1746 (quoting 9 U.S.C. § 2)
[129] *Id.* at 1746
[130] *Sonic-Calabasas A, Inc. v. Moreno, supra,* 57 Cal.4th at 1139
[131] *Id.*
[132] *Id.* (citing *Concepcion, supra,* 131 S.Ct.at 1748, 1751)
[133] *Id.* (citing *Concepcion, supra*, 131 S.Ct. at 1748

---

[134] *Sanchez v. Valencia Holding Co., LLC* (2015) 61 Cal.4th 899, 907

[135] *Id.* at 912

[136] See, e.g., *Armendariz*, supra, 24 Cal.4th at pp. 110–111("[W]hen an employer imposes mandatory arbitration as a condition of employment, the arbitration agreement or arbitration process cannot generally require the employee to bear any type of expense that the employee would not be required to bear if he or she were free to bring the action in court."); *Serpa v. California Surety Investigations, Inc.* (2013) 215 Cal.App.4th 695, 709–710 (*Serpa*) (finding an arbitration agreement unconscionable because it deprived employee of a favorable fee-shifting rule under the Fair Employment and Housing Act (FEHA)); *Ajamian v. CantorCO2e, L.P.* (2012) 203 Cal.App.4th 771, 800 (finding an arbitration agreement unconscionable because it "arguably strips [the employee] of her right to recover attorney fees under her California statutory claims" and "imposes on her the obligation to pay [the employer's] attorney fees where she would have no such obligation under at least one of her California statutory claims"].

[137] *McGill v. Citibank, N.A.* (2014) 232 Cal.App.4th 753, reh'g denied (Jan. 7, 2015) review granted and opinion superseded sub nom. McGill v. Citibank (Cal. 2015); see also *Nelsen v. Legacy Partners Residential, Inc.* (2012) 207 Cal.App.4th 1115, 1136.

[138] *Ferguson v. Corinthian Colleges, Inc.* (2013) 2013 WL 5779514.

[139] *Kilgore v. KeyBank, Nat. Ass'n* (9th Cir. 2013) 718 F.3d 1052.

[140] *Id.* at 463

[141] *Arguelles–Romero v. Sup. Ct.* (2010) 184 Cal.App.4th 825, 836.

[142] *Kinecta Alternative Fin'l Solutions, Inc. v. Sup.Ct. (Malone)* (2012) 205 Cal.App.4th 506, 509–510

[143] *Iskanian v. CLS Transp. Los Angeles, LLC* (2014) 59 Cal.4th 348, 363-364

[144] *Robertson v. Health Net of California* (2005) 132 Cal.App.4th 1419, 1431; *Malek v. Blue Cross of California* (2004) 121 Cal.App.4th 44, 50 (Malek); *Pagarian v. Superior Ct.* (2002) 102 Cal.App.4th 1121, 1151; *Imbler v. PacifiCare* (2002) 103 Cal.App.4th 567, 579; *Smith v. PacifiCare Behavioral Health of Cal., Inc.* (2001) 93 Cal.App.4th 139, 162.
[145] *Medeiros v. Sup. Ct.* (2007) 146 Cal.App.4th 1008, 1017
[146] See *Malek, supra,* 121 Cal.App.4th at 72 ("section 1363.1 is not just a notice statute . . . The signature of the individual enrolling in the health service plan is required in order to ensure a knowing waiver of his or her rights.")
[147] *Id.* at 1015-16
[148] *Id.*
[149] *Id.* at 1020
[150] *Id.* at 1015 (citing *Malek, supra,* 121 Cal. App. 4th at 50)
[151] *Id.* at 1029
[152] *Id.* at 1028
[153] *Id.* at 1029
[154] See *Robertson v. Health Net of California, Inc.* (2005) 132 Cal. App. 4th 1419, 1429; see also *Zembsch v. Superior Ct.* (2006) 146 Cal. App. 4th 153, 165 (despite that arbitration provision set off by a heading, it was not "prominent" because not indented, "bolded, underlined or italicized," and Health Net could have made provision more prominent by using boldface, all capitals and larger fonts)
[155] *Armendariz v. Foundation Health Psychare Services, Inc.* supra, 24 Cal.4th 83, 123-124
[156] *Id.*
[157] *Id.* at 123
[158] *Id.* at 124
[159] *Id.*
[160] *Id.*
[161] *Id.* at 124-125
[162] *Id.*

83084496R00088

Made in the USA
Columbia, SC
08 December 2017